THE MUSHROOM
GUIDE & IDENTIFIER

THE MUSHROOM
GUIDE & IDENTIFIER

An expert manual for identifying, picking and using
edible wild mushrooms found in the British Isles

PETER JORDAN
CONSULTANT: NEVILLE KILKENNY

LORENZ BOOKS

Front endpaper: Oyster mushroom.
Back endpaper: Turkeytail.
Page 1: Trumpet chanterelle.
Page 2: Cep or Penny bun.
Page 3: Wood hedgehog.
Above: Shaggy parasol.
Below right: Pale oyster.
Opposite: Deadly dapperling.

IMPORTANT NOTICE

Careful identification is crucial for all wild
mushroom collecting. You are advised to seek
professional guidance on mushroom forays.
Although many species are edible for many
people, some species cause allergic reactions or
illness to some people; these are unpredictable.
Although the information in the book is believed
to be accurate at the time of going to press,
neither the authors nor publishers can accept any
legal responsibility or liability for the identification
of any mushroom made by users of this guide, nor
for any errors or omissions that may have been
made, nor for any loss, harm or injury that comes
about from following advice in the book.

CONTENTS

FOREWORD

My interest in fungi was stimulated by an inspirational man, Professor Roy Watling – former Head of Mycology and Plant Pathology and one-time Acting Regius Keeper at the Royal Botanic Garden Edinburgh (RBGE), and also former President of the British Mycological Society. I first met Roy on a foraging trip organised by a well-known delicatessen based in Edinburgh and was astonished by his depth of knowledge as he handed out mushrooms for us to smell, cutting ones in half to reveal startling colour changes of blue and red, and putting names to the hundred or so species which we encountered that day. After a couple of years attending forays with Roy, he took me on as an apprentice and taught me mycology for two years at RBGE. He remains a close friend and mentor.

I now lead the same foray, and I am always reminded of Roy's enthusiasm for the foraging community. Foraging connects one to the natural environment, the changing seasons, and the joy of mindfulness. When spared a little time from work and daily chores, nothing brings me greater pleasure than going to look for mushrooms. The time disappears, as your burdens and anxieties slowly give way to exploring familiar habitats: perhaps a damp mossy birchwood shrouding its chanterelle treasure in the dappled light; or a pristine unimproved grassland grazed low by sheep and rabbits to an olive billiard baize ornamented with bright waxcaps. Responsible foragers understand the natural world and care for it. They have a part to play in protecting our environment as well as our ancient foraging culture and should not be underestimated or ignored.

I did not know Peter, but friends that did speak highly of him and it is an honour to be asked to bring his original work up to date. Hopefully it will inspire another forager to take up mycology and immerse themselves in the fungi.

NEVILLE KILKENNY

Left: Trametes versicolor, turkeytail – a charismatic bracket fungus that recycles deadwood; too tough to be edible unless dried and powdered.

INTRODUCTION

I was introduced to wild mushrooms by my grandfather who was a farmer in Norfolk, England. From the age of four I would go out in the fields with him to collect not only what he described as field mushrooms, but also some weird and wonderful-looking mushrooms which I thought were poisonous – they certainly looked menacing to a child. However, he taught me one very good lesson: ensure you can identify with absolute accuracy what you are picking, and you should be safe. From these early beginnings developed a lifetime's interest in wild mushrooms.

The excitement of walking along a woodland path in the autumn, and finding in front of you two or three perfectly formed ceps is wonderful. During fifty years as a mushroom hunter, I graduated from the relatively common horse and field mushrooms to the more exotic chanterelles and ceps. I am still excited when I find the first morels of the spring, or the year's first patch of chanterelles hidden in the leaf mould; of course, the more elusive the mushroom, like horn of plenty or winter chanterelle, the greater the excitement. Imagine the ultimate triumph of finding your first giant puffball – its head often bigger than your own! But, as well as providing excitement and good eating, mushrooms can be dangerous; correct identification is the key to successful mushroom collecting.

The fruits, nuts and mushrooms of autumn are obvious and most are easy to spot. But have you ever realised that the winter, spring and summer can be as productive – at least as far as mushrooms are concerned? Mushrooms are one of the few wild treasures available nearly all the year round. Even on a crisp winter's day you can find a bouquet of silver-grey oyster mushrooms or the wonderful velvet shank growing out of a tree stump, and it is so much more satisfying to pick them like this than from a supermarket shelf. Because, of course, the excitement of finding the mushrooms is followed by the satisfaction of cooking them within hours if not minutes of their harvest.

Identifying mushrooms, utterly essential though it is, can be frustrating if you have to wade through hundreds of illustrations, many of which look the same. This book is designed to make that task easier. It illustrates the best of the edible mushrooms, and so will help you pick your way wisely through the year's mushrooms, alerting you not only to a season's treasures, but also to the poisonous lookalikes and really deadly fungi that all too often grow alongside innocent and delicious mushrooms. The section that deals with the poisonous species will further help identification and give the faint-hearted confidence to take their finds back to the kitchen. But do follow the advice given in this guide carefully. If clear identification is not possible from this book, consult others – the bibliography lists some of the best. And remember that the best advice of all is: if in doubt do not collect a mushroom, and never, ever, eat anything you cannot identify with certainty.

PETER JORDAN

Left: A basket of mushroom bounty from a successful morning's foraging.

WHAT ARE MUSHROOMS?

The kingdom Fungi is now recognised as one of the oldest and largest groups of living organisms. It consists of twelve (previously eight) divisions with an estimated diversity of between 2 and 5 million species. To date, 148,000 species have been formally described with a name, and each year roughly 2,000 more species are described, so over 90% of the Fungi kingdom are still to be named.

The terms mushrooms, toadstools, and fungi (the singular is fungus) are often used loosely and interchangeably. However, this can be misleading. The term fungus refers to the whole persistent organism which is made up of filamentous threads called hyphae. These hyphal threads collectively form a mycelium, a network, that can be found in the soil or other substrates inhabited by the fungus, such as wood and leaf litter. Fungi are neither plants nor animals: they cannot produce their own food like plants, and they cannot ingest food like animals. Instead, they secrete enzymes out into the surrounding environment, breaking down carbohydrates and other complex nutrients

Above: *Fomitopsis betulina*, birch polypore. A medicinal tea can be made from this bracket fungus, although it is of poor flavour.

Below: Many mushrooms grow in rings, some of which reach several metres wide.

which are then absorbed through the hyphal cell wall. They are recognised as a unique kingdom by their non-photosynthetic, absorptive method of feeding, the presence of chitin in their cell walls (a substance also found in insect exoskeletons), their cell membrane chemistry, and their methods of food storage.

The terms mushrooms and toadstools refer to the often ephemeral, short-lived fruiting structures of the fungus. Traditionally we have referred to edible fruiting structures as mushrooms and poisonous ones as toadstools.

However, there are some we call mushrooms that are poisonous and there are also edible toadstools, so the distinction is hardly scientific!

In this book, the term mushroom is used throughout for ease of understanding, whether or not the fruitbody of that particular fungus is edible, and it is used to cover a large number of different types of fruitbodies such as mushrooms, boletes, bracket fungi, puffballs and cup fungi.

TYPES OF FUNGI

As discussed, fungi are neither plants nor animals, but like animals they do require external sources of carbohydrates, which they acquire through a range of ecological strategies.

Saprotroph fungi break down dead organic matter that their mycelium encounters as it grows, such as leaf and needle litter or dead wood. Some fungi can be very specific about what type of organic matter they break down and can be restricted to conifers or broadleaved trees or even particular species.

Mycorrhizal fungi form a symbiotic, mutually beneficial partnership with a plant. The fungus will either sheathe or penetrate the plant's root tips. The surface area represented by the thousands of kilometres of mycelium within the soil vastly increases the potential for nutrient uptake than the plant would be able achieve on its own. In fact, nearly all plants require this partnership to be able take up enough nutrients and moisture to be able to grow, thrive and compete with other plants. In return for these essential mineral nutrients and water that the fungus helps the plant to access, the plant will exchange up to 20% of the carbohydrates it produces by photosynthesis. Again, this relationship can be species specific.

Pathogenic fungi also form a partnership with another organism but derive their nutrition to the detriment of the host. There are many more fungi that are pathogenic to plants than animals, but a particular group of fungi parasitise insects with devastating effect.

It might be fair at this point to ask "why is this in the least bit important to the forager"? Well, you can spend a lot of time searching for mushrooms and be forever disappointed unless you understand that fungi can be very choosy about what type of thing they like to decompose or what type of plant they wish to make partnerships with. For example, you will never find chanterelle or penny bun under sycamore, ash, holly, or rowan, but search under a stand of birch trees, or in an oak or beech wood, and you will greatly improve your chance of success!

FUNGI AS FOOD

Fungi have been used for food and medicine for over 6,000 years. In this book, we focus on a few species. Some of these species are considered to be excellent to eat; others will do us harm, and we demonstrate how to distinguish between the two. One would think that whether a fungus was poisonous or edible would be clear cut, but it is not. Some mushrooms are only edible if cooked, for example. Some fungi can be rendered edible by cooking them in a certain way. We are also unique in ourselves and have our own idiosyncratic reactions to many food types, and this is no different with fungi. A mushroom that one person can eat will not always be tolerated by others. Some people can have severe adverse reactions to eating chanterelles, for instance.

Compared to the huge diversity of fungi that exist, only a few are seriously poisonous and only some are prized as culinary delights. There is a vast diversity of fungi that lie somewhere between mildly poisonous to unpalatable, so it seems best to concentrate on the few that matter. These are the fungi we aim to cover in the book, but it is, of course, not an exhaustive list and you will encounter others in the field.

THE NAMING OF FUNGI

When naming fungi, scientists use the two-name or binomial system, the same used for all organisms, referred to as nomenclature. The first name (which is capitalised) refers to the genus or group to which the organism belongs and the second name (which is lower case) refers to the individual species. Nomenclature has many complicated rules which govern the name attributed to a species.

The science of naming, describing and classifying organisms is called taxonomy and until recently taxonomists studying fungi had no choice but to study only the fruiting body of the fungus, the mycelium being mostly hidden either underground or within the substrate colonised by the fungus. Even if the mycelium could be isolated and studied, there were few characteristics to separate one mycelium from another.

Taxonomists classified fungi using the form and structure characters of the fruiting bodies, and latterly looked at spore shape and ornamentation as the Scanning Electron Microscope (SEM) became available. However, now that molecular tools are available to mycologists, the DNA is revealing links between species and genera which were never considered likely through the morphological studies. This means that fungal nomenclature is in a state of flux far greater than any other group of organisms. The result of this is that names change constantly!

The 'correct' name will be the one first used, depending on where and when it was first published. All other names will be retained as synonyms. To complicate things further, if a taxonomist combines a species with a new genus or into a different old one, this is simply a taxonomic opinion rather than an accepted nomenclatural proposal.

The best way for the forager to deal with this minefield is to retain the name by which they know the fungus and if necessary, for instance when communicating with another, access a website such as Index Fungorum or Mycobank. Simply type the name of your fungus into the search engine and it will give you the current name. In fungal nomenclature, names are often very descriptive, which is useful.

Above: *Parasola plicatilis* (pleated inkcap). This inkcap resembles a minute parasol and is plicate or pleated.

Above: Lichens are a symbiotic association between fungi and algae or cyanobacteria.

ASCOMYCOTA: THE SPORE SPREADERS

Most described species of fungi belong to just two groups, the Ascomycota, comprising approximately 90,000 species, and the Basidiomycota, comprising about 50,000 species. The first group are the 'spore-shooting fungi'; these fungi produce spores in sacs or tubes called asci. The release of the spores is typically triggered by changes in air pressure causing the spores to be 'puffed' out. This can be demonstrated quite dramatically by blowing into some cup fungi such as orange peel fungus. After a brief pause, with a quiet pop, the cup will discharge a cloud of spores into the air.

This Ascomycota group includes the morels, false morels, the true truffles, cup, and saddle fungi. It also includes the asexual unicellular yeasts which reproduce by budding that we use to make beer and bread as well as the moulds that are employed to make blue cheeses and medicines.

The Ascomycota is by far the largest group of fungi and is the dominant group to form a mutualistic, symbiotic partnership with an algae or cyanobacteria which is referred to as lichenisation. 98% of lichen fungi are ascomycetes and about half of all ascomycetes form lichens.

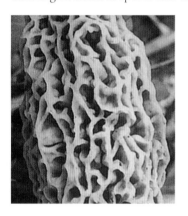

Above: Detail of a common morel.

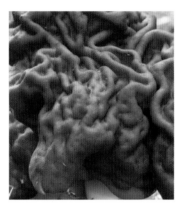

Above: Detail of a false morel.

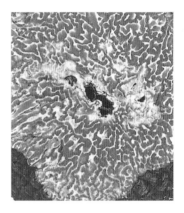

Above: Detail of a true truffle.

Above: Detail of a cup fungus, orange peel.

Above: *Helvella lacunosae*, a saddle fungus.

BASIDIOMYCOTA: THE SPORE DROPPERS

The second group are the 'spore droppers', the Basidiomycota. They produce spores externally on pedestal-type structures called basidia. Their spores are also forcibly discharged by a complex mechanism, but this is much less powerful than that of the spore shooters, and so the spores appear to drop into the moving air. This group includes the umbrella-like fungal fruiting structures that we normally associate with the word mushroom or toadstool. They have a cap that covers and protects the reproductive structures, the gills, which are elevated and supported by a stem. We refer to this type generally as an agaric. The Basidiomycota also includes other similar types of fruiting structures with various types of reproductive surfaces, such as boletes, polypores, chanterelles, hedgehogs, and cauliflowers. The boletes, such as cep, are characterised by having tubes instead of gills and appear 'spongy' underneath. The chanterelles have gill-like wrinkles or veins. The hedgehogs have tiny spines on the underside of the cap, whereas some bracket fungi, the polypores, take their name from their reproductive surface consisting of 'many pores'. The cauliflowers are frondose round structures which broadly resemble the vegetable. In some bracket fungi such as mazegill the pores appear 'stretched' as if aspiring to become gills. In general, these latter groups of the Basidiomycota are easier to distinguish for the beginner than the gilled fungi (the agarics), as there are far fewer of them and they have fewer poisonous lookalikes.

Above: Example of agaric gills.

Above: Example of bolete pores.

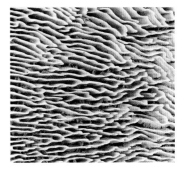

Above: Example of mazegill.

Above: Example of chanterelle decurrent folds or veins.

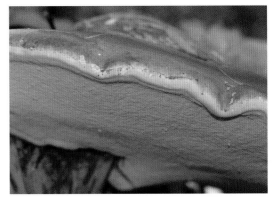

Above: Example of fine layer of pores on birch polypore.

AMANITA

One distinctive and often dangerous group of the agaric fungi is Amanita. These are characterised by growing from a volva, which is the remains of an all-encompassing universal veil. The veil protects the fruitbody from grazing microfauna by covering the fruit body in an egg-shaped bag until the structure starts to grow, whereupon the bag ruptures – sometimes leaving traces of the veil at the base of the stem and on the cap surface. This is what gives the iconic fly agaric, *Amanita muscaria*, its distinctive appearance of contrasting white spots set against the red background of the cap surface. These spots can easily wash off in the rain, however, which can be misleading, so be wary.

The Amanita group includes deathcap, destroying angel and panthercap. Although there are some species considered edible within this group, it should generally be avoided by all but the most experienced foragers, as the consequences of an incorrect identification are potentially fatal.

Sometimes an agaric will have a partial veil which is commonly referred to as a ring – this protects the gills until the fruiting structure begins to mature. As the fruitbody grows, the partial veil breaks away from the cap leaving a ring-like structure on the stem, or shaggy veil around the margin of the cap, or even both. The universal veil and the partial veil (ring) change dramatically as the mushroom develops, making it often look quite different as it ages.

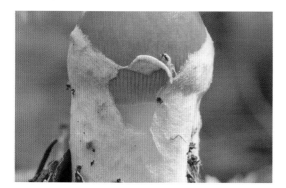

Above: The universal veil still very much in evidence.

Above: *Amanita nivalis* with vaginate volva.

Above: A spotted effect from remains of universal veil.

Above: A distinctive ring or secondary veil.

HOW TO IDENTIFY FUNGI

As the fungal kingdom is so diverse, you need a strategy to navigate through the thousands of species you could potentially encounter to narrow down the identity of what you have before you. It is estimated that there are between 18,000 and 20,000 species of fungi in the UK alone. Luckily, many of these species are what we refer to as microfungi and are of little concern to the forager. To separate between the larger fungi though, we need to closely examine various structures of the fruitbody to first determine its group or genus and then to identify the species.

It is important to record where you have found your mushroom. Was it from a woodland or grassland? Which trees were present? Some fungi are extremely specific about which species they will associate with and will only be found with a certain host. Was it growing in the soil, leaf litter or on wood?

The time of year can be extremely important as well. Traditionally, foraging for fungi is thought of as an autumn activity, but morels appear in the spring, St George's and chicken of the woods in late spring, chanterelle from early summer, and velvet shank over winter.

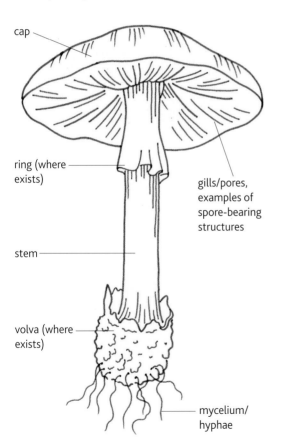

cap

ring (where exists)

gills/pores, examples of spore-bearing structures

stem

volva (where exists)

mycelium/ hyphae

ASCOMYCOTA

The cup fungi circle, enlarged, shows details of the spore-bearing surface.

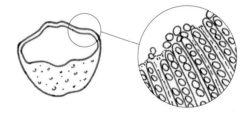

BASIDIOMYCOTA

The gilled mushroom circle, enlarged, shows the enlargement of the gill edge.

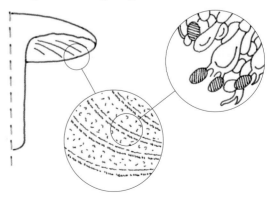

Mushrooms can look quite different as they expand and mature – shapes, sizes and colours can be very variable. Therefore, we must turn to more reliable characteristics, of which the first is the colour of the mushroom's spores (there is a simple technique to establish this on page 20). It's important to collect examples of the mushroom at various ages, to see vital evidence from young specimens as well as being able to get spores from mature ones. Then we need to look at the reproductive structure below the cap – does the mushroom have gills, pores, spines, or wrinkles/folds? We also need to look at whether this structure is protected by anything like a universal veil as in the Amanita group, or a secondary veil or ring, as in the Agaricus group.

In the webcap or Cortinarius group the secondary veil is not a membranous ring but a cottony fibrous web which gives the group its common name.

We should note how the reproductive structure is attached to the cap and the stem. Are the gills 'free' and not touch the stem at all, or do they broadly attach, or are they 'decurrent' and come right down the stem? Have a look at some other types of attachment illustrated here. Note also whether the gills are crowded and close together, or distant, as well as whether they are thick, thin or whether they fork.

The shape of the stem can be very characteristic of some species and it is important to note whether the mushroom is

UNIVERSAL VEIL

marginately
vaginate stem base

stem base with
vaginate volva

stem base with
zoned volva

stem base bare

RINGS OR 'PARTIAL VEILS'

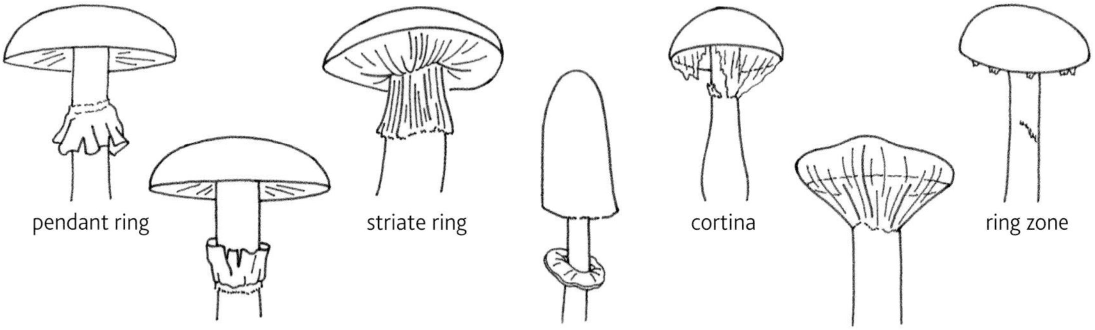

pendant ring

striate ring

cortina

ring zone

peronate ring

moveable
membranous ring

viscid veil

GILL ATTACHMENTS

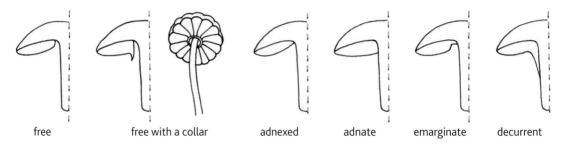

free   free with a collar   adnexed   adnate   emarginate   decurrent

CAP SHAPES

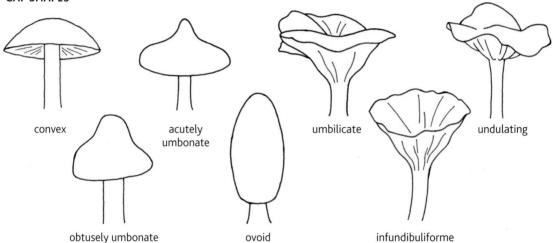

convex   acutely umbonate   umbilicate   undulating

obtusely umbonate   ovoid   infundibuliforme

STEM SHAPES

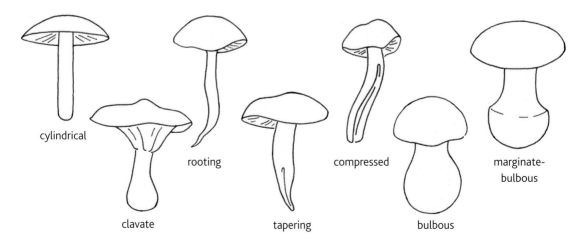

cylindrical   rooting   compressed   marginate-bulbous

clavate   tapering   bulbous

'rooting' down to something in the soil or whether there is a bulb at the base, or evidence of any remains of the universal veil or volva.

Other crucially important characters to record are smells and colour changes. Many fungi have incredibly distinct smells such as coconut, fenugreek, marzipan, aniseed, geraniums, radish, and raw potato, to mention but a few. One type of mushroom is said to smell of old leather and another of oily bed bugs (although some describe it as like carrots)!

Sometimes as you handle mushrooms, they can bruise and discolour. This is particularly relevant in some of the bolete group, where it is also important to cut the mushroom in half to see whether the flesh discolours. Some mushrooms also change colour as they dry out – we call this character 'hygrophanous'. Lastly, you need to examine the cap and stem and note whether they are smooth, fibrous, or scaly.

Fresh, younger specimens exhibit colour changes better and tend to have more noticeable smells. Weather can affect these characteristics dramatically: wind and sun can dry out a specimen, and rain can dilute colour and chemistry, particularly smells.

TASTE

In some groups of mushrooms, taste can be a very important character to assist with identification. Although this can at first seem a little alarming, be assured that it is only used in specific groups of which none are considered seriously toxic. We should also emphasise that tasting is quite different to eating a mushroom and does not involve ingesting any of the fruiting body. One takes a small nibble, chews and then spits out the fragment. The most common groups that require the taste test are brittlegills and milkcaps (with the latter, only the milk should be tasted). The surprise here is that often fungi can taste extremely peppery or acrid – in general we are trying to determine whether

the taste is mild or hot! They can often be very hot, so chew only the tiniest fragment and make sure that you spit it all out. It is wise to keep a water bottle close to hand. You should never automatically taste a mushroom, but if a key asks the question – 'is the taste mild or acrid' – this is when, and only then, to use this identification tool. Other tastes that you may encounter are bitter, rancid, mealy or nutty.

NAVIGATING A 'KEY'

Once you have gathered this identification information you are ready to navigate a 'key' that will hopefully lead you to the name of your mushroom (see pages 22–25). Keys are vital tools to the forager and crucial for foraging with confidence. However, complex keys that cover all the diversity that you are likely to encounter are hard to use and often include complicated terminology that is offputting. Simple keys should be the starting point for the forager, but one must understand that a simple key is just that and cannot account for all eventualities. If a key offers you two options, look up what those options look like, check answers with pictures and descriptions so you understand where the key is trying to lead you, before you make a choice. Consult more than one book! Under some circumstances, you will come to a dead end, effectively 'falling off the key'. If this happens, try again, however if you still come to a dead end, you must discard your mushroom. Another type of key one might encounter is a synoptic key, which works on exclusion and probability, based on the characters fed into it.

When using a key for the first time, the process feels very long-winded. However, as you become familiar with the questions, you will find that you are able to move through quite quickly. The more you use the key, the more likely you are to feel comfortable that you have identified your mushroom correctly. Remember – never eat a mushroom of which the name is unknown.

MAKING A SPORE PRINT

To discern the spore colour, one must make what is called a "spore print". This is done by setting the mature cap of the mushroom down onto a piece of glass, paper or tinfoil and covering it with a cup or bowl to maintain humidity. If you suspect that your mushroom has white-coloured spores, you may want to use a coloured piece of paper rather than white! It is particularly important to not destroy evidence of structures on the mushroom that will help you to identify it, so try to handle it as little as possible and do so gently, holding it in the palm of your hand rather than grasping the stem. Some people separate the cap from the stem to lay it down on the paper, but if you make a hole in the paper or card and drop the stem through it and support the mushroom in a container, all your evidence is left intact. A yogurt pot is perfect for this – you can cut a slot in the lid to rest the specimen on and place another yogurt pot over the top. Better still would be to support your mushroom on two microscope slides in a cup as shown below. After even a few hours, you will see that the spores have fallen from between the gills and onto your glass or paper in a similar pattern to the gills. You will find that the colour will vary from white to cream, pink, light brown, rusty brown, chocolate brown and even black, depending upon which group your mushroom belongs to. Most mushroom guides, as this one, separate by spore colour, often starting with white- and pale-spored mushrooms and ending with dark-spored ones.

1 To take a spore print, support your mature mushroom on glass slides or similar over a small container.

2 A few drops of water in the cup creates humidity. Also, 1–2 drops can be absorbed by the cap, but make sure water does not go on the slide.

3 Cover the container with another to maintain humidity. Leave the mushroom in a warm place for a few hours or overnight.

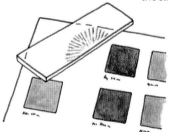

4 The spore print revealed, to be checked against a colour chart for identification.

GLOSSARY OF TERMS

adnate A form of gill attachment, where the gill is broadly attached to the stem.

adnexed A form of gill attachment, where the gills are very narrowly attached to the stem.

Ascomycota Group of fungi characterised by bearing the sexual spores in a sac (asci).

Basidiomycota Group of fungi characterised by the presence of spore-bearing cells called basidia.

brackets Shelf-like fruit bodies, normally without a stem on tree trunks, etc.

cap The portion of the mushroom bearing the gills or tubes, etc.

convex A surface that is curved or rounded outwards.

cortina A cobweb-like partial veil composed of open fibres which connects the edge of the cap to the stem in young fruit bodies.

decurrent A form of gill attachment, where the gills continue down the stem.

emarginate A form of gill attachment, the gills are notched where they meet the stem.

fibrous Composed of or covered in coarse fibres.

flesh The inner hyphae of a fungus within the cap and stem structure.

free A form of gill attachment, where the gills do not touch the stem.

frondose Branching as a broadleaf tree.

fruit body Fungal spore-bearing structure.

gills The blade-like structures on the underside of the cap of a mushroom upon which spores are produced – a hymenium.

heat labile Likely to be altered or degraded when subjected to heat.

Hygrophanous Changing colour depending on moisture in the cap.

hymenium, *pl*. -ia The layer of fertile spore-producing cells (basidia or asci) in Basidiomycota and Ascomycota.

hyphae The very fine, branching filaments that make up the mycelium and fruit bodies of a fungus.

infundibiliform Funnel-shaped.

inrolled Curled inwards.

lateral Referring to the stem being attached to one side of the cap.

marginate Having a distinct margin or border.

milk/latex A fluid usually of milky colour released by some fungi when damaged.

mycelium The collective term for a vegetative mass of hyphae forming a fungus.

network A criss-crossed or reticulate pattern of fine ridges.

partial veil A fine layer of hyphae connecting the cap margin to the stem either as a fragile web or breaking away from the cap to form a ring on the stem.

pores The small openings or mouths of the clustered tubes of boletes and polypores from where the spores are produced.

recurved Curving back, i.e. scales with recurved tips.

ring Remains of the partial veil left on the stem. Evidence of the partial veil may also be found on the edge of the cap.

scales Small to large, raised flakes or flaps of tissue, usually on the cap or stem surface.

spore The sexual reproductive cell of a fungus which may germinate to produce hyphae.

spore print A thick deposit of spores dropped from beneath a mushroom cap on to paper, glass, or foil.

stem The 'stalk' on which a mushroom cap is raised up. Also known as the stipe.

striate With distinct parallel grooves or lines, especially at the cap edge.

tubes The cylindrical units that form the hymenium on boletes and polypores within which spores are produced. The tube openings are the pores.

umbo Raised point or lump in the centre of the cap.

universal veil The fine to thick covering of tissue that envelops the entire fruitbody of some fungi during development.

volva Evidence of the universal veil that remains as a sac, bag, or in some form at the base of the stem.

THE KEY

You will find below a simple key to the mushrooms profiled and referred to in this book. Take the time to explore it, and remember, using a key is the path to safe foraging; trying to just match photographs in books to your specimens is the course towards mushroom poisoning. Once you think you have a name for your mushroom, read the full description of the mushroom that you think you have and make sure it matches exactly with your find. This key should be used in conjunction with the full species descriptions later in the book, as the brief descriptions here do not rule out other mushrooms. It is important to remember that this key only relates to the fungi included in this book and many others will be encountered.

1	**Fruit body is umbrella-like with a cap and a stem – 2.**
	Fruit body is bracket-like on trees – 9.
	Fruit body is of another type – 10.

2	**WITH GILLS:**
	Spores white – off white/cream, includes very pale pink/lilac – 3.
	Spores deep pink – 4.
	Spores milky coffee brown – 5.
	Spores rusty brown – 6.
	Spores dark chocolate brown – 7.
	Spores very dark brown to black – 8.

WITH PORES:

Spores and pores pink – *Tylopilus felleus*, bitter bolete – page 82.

Spores and pores otherwise:
• Pores red – *Rubroboletus satanus*, devil's bolete – page 82. (Warning – there are many red-pored boletes that are not covered in this book.)
• Stem pale with speckles, sometimes dark and contrasting – *Leccinum* spp. – pages 86–87.
• Cap viscid with a ring on stem – *Suillus* spp., slippery jack – pages 88–89.
• Cap viscid when wet, shiny when dry - *Suillus* spp., slippery jack – pages 88–89.
• Cap velvety, cracking, or grainy:
  • Flesh and stem orange to dirty yellow – *Suillus variegatus*, velvet bolete – page 90.
  • Cap cracking red, stem flesh red – *Xerocomellus chrysenteron*, red cracking bolete – page 85.
• Cap matt, smooth:
  • Pores pale yellow, immediately bluing, stem brown – *Imleria badia*, bay bolete – pages 84–85.
  • Pores not bluing, stem white with pale reticulum – *Boletus edulis*, cep or penny bun – pages 82–83.

WITH SPINES – *Hydnum repandum*, wood hedgehog – page 91.

WITH WRINKLES OR SMOOTH – *Cantharellus/Craterellus*, chanterelles – pages 96–101.

3 | **MUSHROOMS WITH GILLS AND WHITE SPORES:**

- Whole fruitbody produces milk/latex when damaged – *Lactarius* spp., milkcaps – pages 62–63, also 140. (Warning – another group, *Mycena* spp., can also produce latex when the stem is broken or cap damaged, but these have much smaller and more delicate fruitbodies.)
- Flesh crumbly, gills normally brittle (exception *Russula cyanoxantha*, charcoal burner), found rarely with intermediate gills which don't reach all the way from the stem to the cap – *Russula* spp., brittlegills – pagess 64–65, also 141.

With a ring:

Gills free:

- With a volva or mealy veil remains at base and veil spots on cap – *Amanita* spp., amanitas – pages 126–35. (Warning – The *Amanitas* covered in this book have rings, but not all do, or not visibly, as with *Amanita* sect. *Vaginatae* which appear not to have a ring.)
- Flesh bruising red/brown on cutting – *Chlorophyllum rhacodes*, shaggy parasol – pages 46–47.
- Large fruit bodies, particularly in grassland, but also woodland and roadsides, with snakeskin pattern on stem, flesh reddens slightly in stem – *Macrolepiota procera*, parasol – page 48.
- Smaller fruit bodies (less than 10cm/4in), caps typically scaly with a low umbo – *Echinoderma/Lepiota* spp., dapperlings – pages 138–39.

Gills decurrent (maybe only slightly):

- Cap honey-coloured, on wood (sometimes buried!), often in large numbers – *Armillaria mellea*, honey fungus – pages 42–43.

Without a ring:

On soil:
Gills adnexed, adnate or emarginate:

- Gills emarginate, cap and stem matt white to cream, appearing late spring, strong mealy smell – *Calocybe gambosa*, St George's mushroom – pages 44–45.
- Caps brightly coloured (red/orange/yellow/green/grey) including white, sometimes viscid, gills thick, sometimes also decurrent. Autumn, in grassland or woodland glades – *Hygrocybe* spp. and allied genera, waxcaps – pages 54–55.
- Caps dull cream, smooth and matt, gills free to adnexed, stem colour as cap, forming rings in grassland late spring to early summer – *Marasmius oreades*, fairy ring champignon – pages 58–59.
- In woodland, gills adnate (sometimes short decurrent), thick and widely spaced:
    - Fruit body purple – *Laccaria amethystina*, amethyst deceiver – page 56.
    - Fruit body cinnamon to buff – *Laccaria laccata*, deceiver – page 57.

Gills decurrent (sometimes short decurrent) – *Clitocybe* spp., funnel cap group – pages 50–51, also 136–37.

On wood:

- Gills free, cap orange, black velvety base to stem, on wood in clusters in winter – *Flammulina velutipes*, velvet shank – pages 52–53.
- Gills deeply decurrent, with short lateral stem – *Pleurotus* ssp., oyster mushroom group – pages 60–61.

4	MUSHROOMS WITH GILLS AND PINK SPORES:

- Gills free, with a volva at base of stem - *Volvopluteus gloiocephalus,* stubble rosegill – not covered in this book.
- Gills free, and on wood, without volva - *Pluteus* spp., shield mushrooms – not covered in this book.
- Gills decurrent with strong mealy smell – *Clitopilus prunulus*, the miller – page 51.
- Gills adnate, emarginate or decurrent, smell perfume-like, fruity or aromatic, not strongly mealy, spores very pale pink – *Lepista* spp., blewit group – pages 66–69.

Warning: All species from *Entoloma* genus have pink spores, with various gill attachments. None are edible.

5	MUSHROOMS WITH GILLS AND MILKY COFFEE SPORES:

- Cap with an umbo, radially fibrous, often splitting at margin – *Inocybe* spp. (Inosperma), fibrecap group – page 143.
- Cap smooth, gills sometimes with brown spots, often smelling of radish or occasionally sweetish – *Hebeloma* spp., poisonpie group – page 142.

6	MUSHROOMS WITH GILLS AND RUSTY BROWN SPORES:

With a ring (sometimes only seen on young fruit bodies):
- On wood, occasionally on soil, sticky to viscid, brown cap with pale to brown fibres on a smooth stem – *Galerina marginata*, funeral bell – page 145.
- On wood, with hygrophanous smooth cap, and stem scaly below ring – *Kuehneromyces mutabilis*, sheathed woodtuft (an edible mushroom often mistaken for funeral bell and vice versa) – not covered in this book.

With a cortina or web (sometimes only seen on young fruit bodies): *Cortinarius* spp., webcaps – page 144.

Without a ring or web:
- Gills decurrent, cap edge inrolled – *Paxillus involutus*, brown rollrim – pages 146–47.
- Small delicate mushrooms in soil and on wood with brown striate caps – *Galerina* spp., funeral bell group – page 145.
- Small delicate mushrooms on soil and on wood with non-striate brown caps – *Conocybe* spp., conecap group – not covered in this book.

7	Mushrooms with gills and dark chocolate brown spores:

- With a ring – *Agaricus* spp., true mushroom group – pages 70–79, also 148–49.

8	MUSHROOMS WITH GILLS AND VERY DARK BROWN OR BLACK SPORES:

With a ring:
- Liquefying to a black inky mess – *Coprinus comatus*, shaggy inkcap/lawyer's wig – pages 80–81.
- Not liquefying, cap with green tones – *Stropharia aeruginosa*, verdigris roundhead – page 50.

Without a ring:

On soil, liquefying to a black inky mess:
- Pale scales on contrasting dark background – *Coprinopsis picacea*, magpie inkcap – page 80, also 150.
- Cap grey without contrasting scales – *Coprinopsis atramentaria*, common inkcap – page 150.

8	On wood:

- Cap and stem yellow, in clustered tufts, gills grey/green – *Hypholoma fasciculare*, sulphur tuft – page 151.
- Cap with red/brown tones, gills yellow – *Hypholoma lateritium*, brick tuft – page 151.

9	**FRUIT BODY IS BRACKETLIKE ON TREES:**

Bracket with frondose-stemmed lobes:
- Not bruising black – *Grifola frondosa*, hen of the woods – pages 106–07.

Bracket not with frondose-stemmed lobes:
- Bracket bright yellow, found mostly on oak, willow or cherry (occasionally yew) – *Laetiporus sulphureus*, chicken of the woods – pages 108–09.
- Bracket red/brown, on oak – *Fistulina hepatica*, beefsteak fungus – pages 104–05.
- Grey-brown, bruising black – *Meripilus giganteus*, giant polypore – page 107.
- Cap with scales, with short lateral stem, pores decurrent and smelling of watermelon – *Cerioporus squamosus*, dryad's saddle – pages 102–03.
- Cap felty with yellow margin on the base and roots of conifer trees – *Phaeolus schweinitzii*, dyer's mazegill – page 109.
- Bracket on dead birch, underside white appearing smooth when young – *Fomitopsis betulina*, birch polypore/razorstrop fungus – depicted pages 10 and 14.

10	**FRUIT BODY OF ANOTHER TYPE:**

- Fruit body with stem and pitted honeycomb-like head, head and stem form a single hollow chamber – *Morchella* spp., morels – pages 112–15.
- Fruit body with a stem and wrinkled convoluted head, stem and head form several individual chambers – *Gyromitra esculenta*, false morel – page 113.
- Fruit body spherical, hemispherical or pestle-shaped, white inside when young, becomes greenish with a thin outer wall – *Lycoperdon/Apioperdon/Calvatia* spp., puffballs – pages 94–95.
- Fruit body spherical, hemispherical or pestle-shaped, hard, marbled black inside with a thick outer skin – *Scleroderma* spp., earthballs – page 95.
- Fruit body roughly spherical, black and below ground – *Tuber aestivum*, summer truffle – page 117.
- Fruit body spherical to hemispherical, frondose like a cauliflower – *Sparassis crispa*, cauliflower fungus – pages 110–11.
- Fruit body cup-shaped, cup facing down, either soft or brittle (drying out), tan to dark brown, hanging from fallen and attached branches – *Auricularia auricula-judeae*, jelly ear – pages 92–93.
- Fruit body cup-shaped, cup facing up on soil and woody debris, various colours black, dull brown to yellow, *Peziza spp.* and other members of the *Pezizaceae* – page 93.
- Fruit body cup-shaped, cup facing up on soil/buried woody debris, but bright orange, often quite flattened – *Aleuria aurantia*, orange peel fungus – pages 116–17.

It is important to remember that this key only relates to the fungi included in this book and many others will be encountered – also see other recommended reading at the back of the book.

WHERE AND WHEN TO COLLECT MUSHROOMS

Where to collect fungi and where you are allowed to collect are two separate questions and the former may be the easier to answer than the latter!

The Theft Act 1968 which covers England and Wales declares "A person who picks mushrooms growing wild on any land, or who picks flowers, fruit or foliage from a plant growing wild on any land, does not (although not in possession of the land) steal what he picks, unless he does it for reward or for sale or other commercial purpose." Some local by-laws can be contradictory to this, but these should always be clearly signposted: Epping Forest where the collection of fungi is banned is one example of this. The Countryside and Rights of Way Act 2000 essentially grants unrestricted access to designated areas of the countryside. This includes upland areas, downlands, heath and mountain, as well as land voluntarily opened up by a landowner. However, if you attempt to access private land (the majority of land in England and Wales is privately owned) you are committing the civil offence of trespassing.

Below: Mature wet birch woodland can be very rewarding for fungi.

It is of note that the Theft Act and the National Trust by-laws, for instance, refer to fungi specifically. Some confusion often arose in the past when similar legislation was introduced, as fungi were still at that time considered to be plants. It was not until 1969 that Roger Whittaker proposed a fifth kingdom to accommodate fungi.

The Land Reform (Scotland) Act 2003 enshrined the 'Right to Roam', previously supported by the absence of the offence of trespass in Scottish Law, unlike elsewhere in the UK. However, under Scottish common law, plants and fungi are included in the 'parts and pertinents' to land, making the produce of the land the property of the owner. So, it would appear that in most of England and Wales you have the right to collect fungi, but not to be there in the first place, except on common land (subject to by-laws). Whereas in Scotland, you have the right to be there, but not to pick!

Interestingly the Land Reform (Scotland) Act is silent regarding gathering produce for non-commercial purposes, almost purposely leaving the legal status of such activities ambiguous. Long-established rights often override formal legal measures, harvesting is hard to police and the laws themselves are difficult to implement. Therefore, the reality is that so long as you do not trespass and you are collecting what is considered a reasonable amount for personal use (The Wild Mushroom Pickers' Code of Conduct suggests that 1.5kg per visit is reasonable and would, I suggest, suffice for most families), you are unlikely to be challenged. If in doubt, always ask the landowner's permission. You must ask permission if you intend to organise wild food walks or collect for commercial gain. Although this is permitted in Scotland under the Scottish

Right: Early morning is prime mushroom hunting time.

Outdoor Access Code, it is still polite to ask and avoids clashes with other events in the same locality. You should avoid collecting in nature reserves generally unless the reserve actively promotes foraging. It is illegal to collect fungi from a Site of Special Scientific Interest and a National Nature Reserve in Scotland. It is illegal for anyone, including the landowner, to collect a species listed in the Schedule 8 category under the Wildlife and Countryside Act 1981.

So, this now leads on to the opening question. When is it best to pick? This will be governed by the time of year and depends on what you are looking for. As the reader will know by now, having read this far, many fungi are extremely specific to certain habitats and times of year. There is an annual rhythm to mushroom fruiting, and it is important for the forager to attune themselves to this natural progression. Velvet shank, jelly ear and oyster mushrooms can be found on large fallen broadleaf branches or dead standing trunks over winter, and in damp, broadleaved woodland with base-rich soil, scarlet elf cups are the red jewels against a lush green background from late autumn to early spring. Just as we say farewell to these, morels appear. Black morels appear to prefer coniferous woodlands, disturbed soils, wood chip and burn sites,

whereas *Morchella esculenta* prefers broadleaf woodland with sandy and chalky soils. Next up are St George's mushrooms, taking their name from the date they are expected to appear. These frequent chalky grassland and woodland fringes and are swiftly followed by fairy ring champignon which are easy to identify from the darker circles of luxuriant growth in lawns and pastures. Dryad's saddle and chicken of the woods can now be found on tree trunks.

Early summer is often punctuated by some field mushrooms in grassland and the first chanterelle in wet areas of woodland. As we move into late summer, the boletes appear in our woodlands and are soon joined by a swell of fungal diversity with mycorrhizal and recycling saprotroph species carpeting our woods, and parasols, waxcaps and other *Agaricus* species decorating our fields. Late autumn brings with it wood blewits and later still field blewit, and so the cycle turns full circle.

The ebbs and flows of this cycle will naturally be led by the weather, and prolonged dry periods will mean that the forager will have to search out the damper habitats, river gorges and valleys. Occasionally, if the host plant to the fungus is stressed by drought, this can provoke a vigorous production of fruiting bodies by the fungus. A

Below: The St George's mushroom traditonally appears around 23rd April, St George's Day.

Below: Chicken of the woods grows from late spring to early autumn.

sharp early frost can have a similar effect. In general, however, it normally takes ten days to a fortnight for fungi to respond to rain after long dry periods. Understanding the phenology of your environment is important and rather than recording just a date in your diary, it is worth noting if it is the same time as the swallows arrived or the beech leaves unfurled from their cigar-like buds, or if the appearance of your mushroom coincided with the squirrels busying themselves storing seeds from pine cones. These are more reliable indicators of when is the 'right time' for a mushroom to be in season.

In general, one would expect to see greater diversity in older woodlands and undisturbed grasslands. Chicken of the woods, beefsteak fungus and hen of the woods are considered indicators of ancient oak woodland. An old damp stand of birch trees will be rewarding for chanterelles, and mature beech woods will often provide large quantities of wood hedgehogs. Mature pinewoods are home to cauliflower fungus and several species of slippery jack, as well as ceps (penny buns). Millers are probably parasitic on the mycorrhiza of ceps and their tree host, and where one is found the other will be also, although not always at the same time. Fly agarics share a similar habitat preference to ceps

and can also be used as an indicator. Ceps are not restricted to pinewoods though, and flourish well in Sitka spruce plantations and mature beech and birch stands.

Common names of mushrooms are often a good clue as to the type of woodland in which they are to be found. Brown birch bolete and oak milkcap are a couple of good examples. As one becomes familiar with the different species, you will soon recognise where one should look for them. Remember also, as mentioned earlier, that only certain types of tree form symbiotic partnerships with the type of fungi which produce mushroom and toadstool type fruiting structures, so choose your woodland accordingly.

The forager also needs to keep in mind other factors. Is the shrub or grassland likely to have been sprayed with a pesticide? Shaggy inkcaps like disturbed soils which could potentially be contaminated. They are often seen in farm stackyards for instance. Mushrooms are often prolific along roadsides, and indeed any form of boundary: the mycelium hits the edge of its potential territory and the natural response to such a threat is to reproduce. Consider whether mushrooms close to roadsides could have picked up pollutants from motor vehicles, or whether dogwalkers are also using a pathway.

Below: Wood blewits appear later in the season, autumn to early winter.

Below: Oyster mushrooms continue to grow through the winter.

HOW TO COLLECT MUSHROOMS

First and foremost, safety is, of course, of upmost importance. You should always consider your own safety. Newspapers report occasionally of collectors in Italy heading out before dawn so they can reach their 'patch' unseen, only to be discovered later, at best only injured, at the foot of some mountain precipice. You should dress for the weather and the terrain. Particularly on longer walks and in areas where you are not familiar, a map and compass can be useful; a phone can be out of signal range (or run out of battery). It is important to regularly locate your position as you will be meandering through the terrain staring mainly at the ground and it is quite easy to get disorientated. It is worth checking the weather forecast before setting off and checking for the existence of livestock wherever you venture.

RESPECTFUL FORAGING
Picking mushrooms is a time-honoured pastime; many of us have memories of mushroom foraging with a basket. However it is important to be careful in your picking, and to be aware of the issues of sustainability to ensure the continuation of the wild mushrooms. Avoid damaging the mycelium of the fungus as much as possible. Check local restrictions and environmental laws, which can vary.

On a good day, in a local area that you are familiar with, little equipment is required other than a knife and something to carry your collections in. A wicker basket is ideal, but you could also use an old supermarket basket or

Left: A morning's bounty: a basket full of charcoal burners, wood hedgehogs, chanterelles, trumpet chanterelles, horn of plenty, cep, millers and princes.

Below: A good folding knife is essential, and some double as a brush as well.

even a food-safe plastic container. It is important not to seal your plastic tub though, as it can encourage your mushrooms to start to sweat and decay. Similarly, plastic bags should be avoided; not only are they a catalyst for deterioration, but your mushrooms will get knocked and squashed and soon become a mixture of crumbled fragments that are impossible to differentiate. A roll of aluminium foil is useful to separate out specimens you have yet to identify, folding them carefully into little parcels to protect them and to keep them apart from other pickings.

You will need to collect all the evidence available to identify your mushroom, so carefully pluck or ease out the mushroom from the soil to retain any information from the base of the stem. One should not over-handle the mushroom either. Important structures such as rings and veils can become damaged or removed which can make the specimen impossible to identify. Your knife ideally would be one designed for mushrooming, with a curved blade to reach around the stem and a brush on the back to remove any excess soil.

You will need a good guidebook to refer to, one that is specific to the region that you are collecting in. Never collect more than a few examples for identification if you are not conversant with a species. Never eat a mushroom if you cannot confidently identify it.

Fungal toxins can be passed through the skin if one is handling a lot of poisonous fungi, but normally there is little risk from handling mushrooms. Soil contains many bacteria, however, so maintaining good hygiene is important. Some hand gel is a good precaution.

If you are already familiar with the species you are collecting, you can confidently trim the stem to remove any soil debris and brush the cap to get rid of any other foreign bodies – if you clean as you go, it will save you hours later – and then pick your mushroom.

Now we come to the controversial question! To cut or to pluck? Some argue that plucking your specimen from the soil can damage the mycelium and that often at the base of the stem a button or pin mushroom can be seen ready to replace the mushroom you have collected. Others suggest that a stump offers a huge open wound for bacteria to work down into the mycelium, threatening the entire organism. Grazing animals are less conscientious and eventually all mushrooms will rot down anyway, so the bacteria argument is possibly unsubstantiated. Personally, I find cut stumps unappealing and contrary to the woodland's aesthetic and prefer to carefully pluck and then trim, scattering cuttings discretely. In general, one should be light-handed and light-footed (soil compaction is a greater threat to fungi than mushroom picking). You should leave no trace of your visit, leaving as many mushrooms as you take or perhaps graze foraging, taking a few here, a few there, so that there is minimum impact on the natural resources for other biodiversity and for other visitors.

You should leave old specimens that are past their best, using the judgement of 'would I want to' rather than 'can I', eat it. Fungus gnat larvae are often prolific in older specimens, and mould or bacterial infections are not uncommon. You should never collect 'button' mushrooms which have yet to reach maturity and release spores. This is a self-depreciating exercise often seen when people compete over a patch. If the fungus has no opportunity to release its spores, even if as research suggests, collecting mushrooms has little effect on the existing organism, it will affect the potential of the fungus to spread to other areas and proliferate. Keep in mind that 'your patch' could well have previously been discovered by another, who may also feel it is 'their patch'. Remember the joy of encountering your first patch of chanterelle (for instance), and leave some mushrooms for someone else.

MUSHROOMS IN THE KITCHEN

Wild mushrooms have been valued for centuries in the kitchen. From the cook's point of view, they are an irresistible source of flavour, texture and aroma. Even if you've only managed to find a few mushrooms, they will go a long way to flavour a plate, and they are prized to bulk a dish as an alternative for meat.

If cooking fresh, simple preparation is needed to ensure the mushroom is clean (dirt- and maggot-free), and hints and tips for handling the different types of fungi are given here. There are also certain times of the year when mushrooms grow in great profusion and you want ways to preserve this abundance for when there are fewer pickings to be had. Preserving food is as old as time itself and, long before refrigerators, salting and drying were used as methods of preservation. There are many different ways to store mushrooms and some species are more suited to a certain type of preservation than others. Information on the most suitable method for each species is given in the relevant directory entry.

RAW OR COOKED
Although some cultivated mushrooms are eaten raw, recent research suggest that all mushrooms should be cooked. Heat will destroy carcinogens that are common in cultivated and wild mushrooms. Several species of wild mushroom also contain heat-labile toxins, which are destroyed by cooking at high temperatures. Mushrooms such as honey fungus *Armillaria mellea*, chicken of the woods *Laetiporus sulphureus*, wood blewit *Lepista nuda*, field blewit *L. personata* and the morels *Morchella elata* and *M. esculenta* all contain these toxins, which are destroyed by thorough cooking.

Whatever method of storage you are going to use, it is important to select the very best of the mushrooms you have collected. Do be careful to make sure that they are completely free of maggots and other insects because there is nothing worse when reconstituting dried mushrooms to find you have insects floating on the top of the water in which they are being reconstituted. Also make sure there are no twigs, leaves or other debris among them.

Below: Ceps are firm and sturdy but also absorbent, so it's best to use a wet cloth to wipe any dirt away.

The pores underneath the cap are tightly woven, so usually just need a quick brush or wipe over.

PREPARING AND CLEANING MUSHROOMS

Cooks tend to apply a one-rule-for-all policy when it comes to mushrooms, but this can mean that you spoil a dish by washing the super-absorbent cep or trying vainly to brush a mud-caked horn of plenty. Some mushrooms need a gentle bath, some wiping with a wet cloth, and others just a quick dust with a dry brush. As you use different mushrooms, it will become apparent how best to tackle them, depending on how delicate they are, whether they are gilled or pored, how and where they grow – and of course how dirty they are.

Below: Cauliflower fungus can be full of bugs and dirt, but sturdy enough to wash in lukewarm water.

After you have washed it, hold the mushroom over paper and lightly tap out remaining bits of debris.

Below: The saffron milkcap can have brittle-dry gills so carefully brush out dirt with a dry brush.

You can then wipe the tops and stalks with a clean damp cloth or piece of kitchen paper.

DRYING MUSHROOMS

Drying preserves the flavour and colour quite well, although unfortunately it often destroys the shape of the mushroom. There are several methods. In warmer climates, slicing the mushrooms and laying them on muslin (cheesecloth) trays in the sun can be quite sufficient. In cooler, less sunny regions, mushrooms can be dried on open trays in an airing cupboard, and on windowsills – they need to be placed somewhere warm, dry and ventilated. The mushrooms should be dried quickly after picking, and thoroughly, which should take a few hours but may take longer. It is possible to use a very low oven (about 50°C/112°F) with the door ajar.

In recent years, fruit dryers and drying machines have become available. Some can take up to ten trays and are capable of drying a large quantity of wild mushrooms very effectively over several hours. The advantage of this is that it prevents the whole house smelling of mushrooms for days afterwards, and you can also be totally confident that your mushrooms are completely free of moisture. With this accelerated form of drying it is possible to dry even shaggy ink caps, so long as you use very young specimens. Ordinary drying methods are much too slow and they would collapse into an inky mess and probably ruin any other mushrooms you were drying with them.

Another effective way of drying mushrooms is to thread them with a needle and cotton and hang them up in strings in the kitchen. It is important to remember, however, that mushrooms such as morels could well have creepy-crawlies hiding inside so partially dry them somewhere food-free before hanging them in your kitchen.

When the mushrooms are dry, carefully lay them on a sheet and pick the individual specimens over before placing them in airtight containers for storage. Don't waste any powder that may remain on the sheet; it can be stored separately and used to flavour soups and stews.

Dried mushrooms can be put directly into soups and stews, but for other dishes it is best to reconstitute them in lukewarm water for around twenty minutes. Do not use boiling water as this will impair the final flavour. The water in which they have been reconstituted can be used as stock or to make gravy, but, before you do so, pour it through a sieve or filter to remove any extraneous matter or grit.

Below: A mushroom drier has ventilated layers to dry a large number of cleaned and sliced mushrooms.

Below: To bring dried mushrooms back to life, soak them in warm, not boiling, water for 20 minutes.

Above and below: Slice the clean mushrooms then place them on a basket tray somewhere warm and dry.

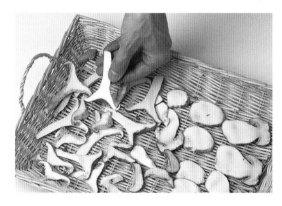

Below: When completely dry, transfer the mushrooms into an airtight clean, dry jar and store in a dark place.

PICKLING

Small mushrooms can be pickled in either oil or vinegar. It is most important when using this method to clean the mushrooms well and then blanch them. Make sure the containers you use are well-sterilised, have a good seal, and when they are filled, sealed tightly.

Remember that the better the vinegar or oil used, the better the results will be. Bring about 250ml/8fl oz vinegar and 150ml/¼ pint of water to a simmer in a pan and add a teaspoon of salt and spices or dried herbs if using (perhaps a red chilli, and a couple of teaspoons of coriander seeds and anise pepper). Add the mushrooms (about 250g/9oz for vinegar pickles and 450g/1lb for oil) and simmer for 10–15 minutes, then allow to cool. For vinegar pickles, decant both the mushrooms and liquid into the jar. For oil pickles, drain the mushrooms and dry thoroughly before putting them into the jar with about 400ml/14fl oz olive oil.

Use within 6 months. Once the seals have been broken, use the contents fairly quickly, and keep the container in the fridge. Keep a watchful eye on your pickled mushrooms for any sign of mouldiness. If there is, discard the top few mushrooms and use up the rest quickly.

Below: Use a good-quality olive oil for pickling your mushrooms, as the flavour will shine through.

FREEZING

An alternative to drying is freezing. It isn't always successful but the firmer varieties of mushroom are best, such as St George's, blewits, horn of plenty, chanterelle, and closed field and horse mushrooms.

Ensure they are free from grit and infestation then trim and slice quickly if large, before blanching (or frying), open-freezing and then freezing in portion-sized bags. Label them with type and date; they will keep in the freezer for up to about 6 months. To thaw, immerse briefly in boiling water before using.

Below: Bring a pan of salted water to the boil and blanch the mushrooms for about 1 minute. Drain well.

Open-freeze for 30–40 minutes on a tray lined with greaseproof-paper, before storing in freezer bags.

SALTING

Salting is one of the oldest methods of preserving and works extremely well for mushrooms. The most important thing is to have clean, fresh mushrooms. The quantities required are one part salt to three parts mushrooms. Layer the mushrooms and salt alternately, and make sure the final layer of mushrooms is completely covered with salt. Use containers that the salt will not corrode. A sterilised glass jar is best, but you could also use plastic containers. You will not need to add salt in any dish you make using these mushrooms.

Below: Alternate layers of rock or sea salt with cleaned, sliced mushrooms, packing in until the jar is full.

After 3–4 hours you will find the volume of mushrooms has dropped; add exra layers to fill.

MUSHROOM POWDER

The intense flavour of dried mushrooms can be used in powder form to enliven stocks, winter soups, stews and curries. The curry-scented milkcap, *Lactarius camphoratus*, offers a pungent reminder of fenugreek, though use it sparingly. (Also, be careful not to confuse it with the *Lactarius helvus*, fenugreek milkcap!) The aniseed funnel mushroom, *Clitocybe odora*, is another powerful substitute for spices and can be used in sweet and savoury cooking. Others suitable for powdering include many of the boletes, and field and horse mushrooms.

Below: Wipe a coffee grinder clean, put in the well-dried mushrooms, and reduce to a fine powder.

Transfer the powder to a clean airtight jar, label and keep in a dark place. Use sparingly.

MUSHROOM EXTRACT

The finest mushrooms are best preserved whole or sliced, but some such as the field, horse and parasol mushroom lend flavour and colour to a dark extract. It is very important to ensure mushrooms are properly identified before using. Shaggy inkcaps can be worth adding, as are any overgrown (edible) boletus in good condition. For 450g/1lb mushrooms add 300ml/½ pint water, 200ml/7fl oz red wine, 60ml/4 tbsp soy sauce, 5ml/1 tsp salt and a sprig of thyme. The extract will keep in the fridge for 8–10 weeks. Use to enliven stocks, soups and stews.

Below: Simmer everything for 45 minutes, then press through a sieve. It is the liquid that is retained.

Boil down the liquid until reduced to half, then pour into sterilised bottles, or ice cube trays to freeze.

EDIBLE MUSHROOMS

A lot of people are passionate about foraging for many types of food these days. It provides a reconnect with the landscape and passing seasons that we feel our hectic lives have dragged us away from. Wild mushrooms often feature at the top of the list of greatly desired foraged foods, possibly because of the mystique that surrounds them.

Despite the excitement of picking mushrooms in the wild, there is the ever-prevalent risk of collecting poisonous species by mistake. Wild mushrooms should be treated with the respect that they deserve, and a thorough approach should be adopted in the process of identification. Mistakes, as history demonstrates, can be fatal. Use this section in conjunction with the next, which highlights some of the poisonous lookalikes you might come across. Always use a key to identify your mushrooms; never just compare with pictures as fungi have notoriously little respect for size, shape or colour! Focus on reliable characters such as spore colours, evidence of veils and gill attachments. Whenever possible, accompany someone who knows which mushrooms are safe and remember, if in doubt, leave it out!

Left: *Leccinum versipelle*, orange birch bolete – a choice edible mushroom, but one known to cause stomach upsets if undercooked.

SAFE MUSHROOMING

This section illustrates and describes some of the best mushrooms considered to be edible that grow in our fields and woods. It is estimated that between 300 and 1,000 species in Europe are considered edible, but only a small proportion, perhaps 100, of these are prized for their flavour and texture. Approximately 65 of the most common and popular varieties have been selected or referred to in this directory.

To enable identification each entry has a detailed description of the species in question and information on its habitat and season of growth. Storage and cooking suggestions are also offered specific to each type of mushroom, as a number lend themselves better to some processes and preparations than others.

As you learn about mushrooms you will become more respectful of the rules of identification. No mushroom looks exactly like another. This will become obvious when you apply the correct degree of scrutiny. You will also notice that sometimes you will see great variation within the same species because of age, weather conditions and surrounding vegetation. Many species have poisonous lookalikes, which are also mentioned here and described in further detail in the next section. Particular care should be taken in the identification of such mushrooms. When collecting specimens for identification it is important to get examples which represent all stages of growth, from very young with any evidence of veils and ring intact, to fully mature specimens that demonstrate the final shape and colour of the cap from which a spore print can be taken. Only with all stages of development can you be sure of an accurate identification. At first, try to restrict yourself to just a few species.

Enjoy your mushroom collecting, but do not take any risks with mushrooms that you cannot identify. Even the ones you can identify may cause unexpected reactions. Remember that some people can eat things that others cannot. As with shellfish, we can have our own personal reactions to different fungi. Mushrooms can be quite rich and even edible ones can cause stomach upsets. Some people appear more prone to these than others, so be careful if you are serving a mushroom dish to guests. A good example of this is chicken of the woods. The chemistry in young and older fruitbodies has been found to be quite different; older fruitbodies have been known to cause stomach upsets and only young growth should be collected as food.

The fungi discussed in this book include those that are generally considered either edible (if cooked correctly) or poisonous. However, as each person is different, only you, the reader, will be able to determine whether a fungus is edible or not, for you. If you choose to eat a fungus described in this book, you do so at entirely your own risk. If you are eating a mushroom for the first time, try only a small amount – the severity of a fungal poisoning is directly related to the amount of toxin consumed. Do not mix a new species with other mushrooms. Always keep a specimen back, so that you have something to take with you to hospital for a mycologist to identify.

Left: Chicken of the woods, *Laetiporus sulphureus,* is a tasty mushroom that arrives early in the season. It must be thoroughly cooked and only the freshest young growth should be collected.

HONEY FUNGUS OR BOOT-LACE FUNGUS
Armillaria mellea

Honey fungus is the dreaded enemy of the gardener. This mushroom grows from black cords known as rhizomorphs which can travel enormous distances. They kill the host tree and infect large areas of woodlands.

The name honey fungus refers to quite a wide suite of species which associate with both broadleaved and coniferous trees, though not all species are vigorous parasites. However, for the mushroom hunter, honey fungus is extremely good to eat and grows in very large quantities during the autumn. They can grow in large clumps or individually, either on dead tree trunks, tree stumps or living coniferous and broadleaf trees.

Above: The scales of the cap vary considerably, ranging from almost smooth, as seen here, to quite coarse.

IDENTIFICATION
The cap can range from 2–8cm/¾–3in across, mostly olive yellow with a greyish-brown centre with brown scales. It starts by being convex, then flattens and is centrally depressed. The fruitbodies grow in huge bundles of up to 25 or more. The stem is 0.4–1cm/¼–½in wide and 5–15cm/2–6in long, slender with a membranous ring. The gills are slightly decurrent and vary from off-white to brown. The flesh is white with an astringent smell. The spore print is off-white.

HABITAT AND SEASON

Armillaria mellea is fairly widespread in deciduous woods, infecting living trees as well as dead trunks and stumps. The season lasts from early summer to early winter and they can appear several times at the same place during a season.

STORAGE

Drying tends to toughen this mushroom, so it is best to make up dishes first and then freeze them, if not eating straight away.

PREPARATION AND COOKING HINTS

Only the caps are edible – the stalks are very tough. It is usually blanched before cooking, to avoid any allergic reaction; boil the caps for 2–3 minutes in lightly salted water, which must then be discarded as the mushroom may contain a mild toxin. Then cook as you wish. After the initial blanching, the caps are good sautéed with

Above: Honey fungus mushrooms tend to grow in large clumps, typically in clusters of 25 or more.

onion, garlic and basil, thickened with a little cream and served with pasta. Honey fungus can lose its texture after cooking and the flavour is an acquired taste for some, however.

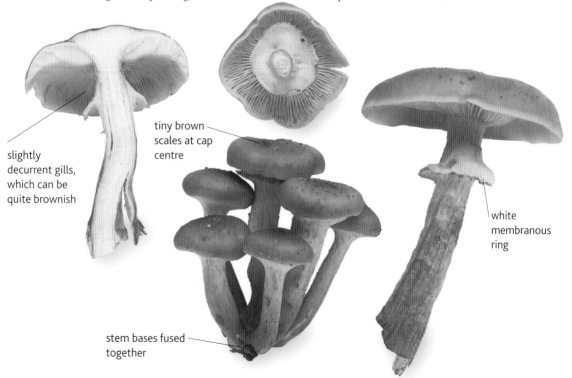

slightly decurrent gills, which can be quite brownish

tiny brown scales at cap centre

white membranous ring

stem bases fused together

ST GEORGE'S MUSHROOM
Calocybe gambosa

As its name suggests, St George's mushroom tends to appear around 23rd April, St George's Day (and Shakespeare's birthday). It has a great variety of uses and is particularly welcome because it appears early in the year, usually just after the morel. It frequently grows in rings which can be very large, although broken in places. The largest rings may be several hundred years old.

IDENTIFICATION
The cap is 4–11cm/1½–4¼in across with a slightly inrolled margin, and always feels cold. Well-rounded when young, large old specimens develop an irregular, wavy cap. It is white to cream in colour. The stem is 3–9cm/1¼–3½in

Above: In these mature specimens note how the caps are irregular and wavy.

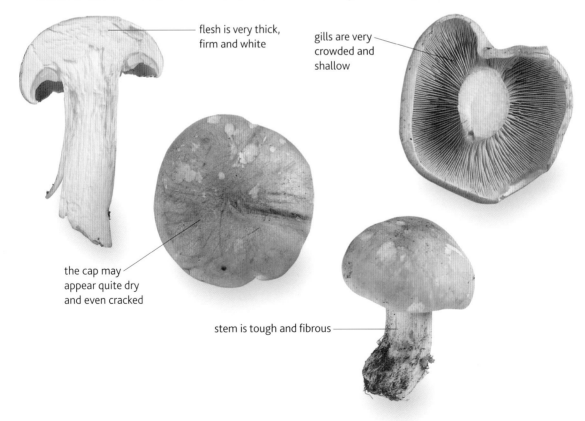

flesh is very thick, firm and white

gills are very crowded and shallow

the cap may appear quite dry and even cracked

stem is tough and fibrous

Above: The caps vary from chalky white to a creamy yellow colour, but always have a strong mealy smell.

long and 1–3cm/½–1¼in across, and white. The ivory gills are emarginate, narrow and crowded. The white and soft flesh has a pleasant mealy smell. The spore print is white.

HABITAT AND SEASON
Tends to grow in rings in grassy locations, and likes old pasture and areas around wood edges with underlying chalk. The season is from the beginning of April and into May. For good growth St George's mushroom relies on warmth and moisture, so if the spring is cold it will not appear until the weather turns warmer. (Early St George's mushrooms are often cold to the touch which reflects the late spring soil temperature.) Keep checking areas where you have seen it before as you will find new pickings in the same spot. When picking this mushroom always twist, pluck and then cut the stem.

STORAGE
St George's mushroom dries extremely well. It can also be stored in olive oil or in vinegar.

PREPARATION AND COOKING HINTS
Both young and older specimens are good in cooking; the texture is quite firm and dry and the taste slightly mealy. Brush the caps well because they can be quite gritty and dirty and there may be chalk particles on the undersides. It goes particularly well with chicken and fish.

SHAGGY PARASOL
Chlorophyllum rhacodes

Previously known as *Macrolepiota rhacodes*, this was once thought a variant of the larger parasol (page 48) but has since been reassigned to a different family. Although it is edible it can cause stomach upsets.

IDENTIFICATION
The grey to brown cap, 6–18cm/2½–7in diameter, is ovate at first and then expands and flattens out, cracking to form uplifted scales against a white background. The gills are free and remote from the stem, and crowded. It has a thick double layered ring which is moveable up and down the stem. The smooth pale stem, 3–20cm/1¼–8in long and 0.7–3cm/¼–1¼in broad, has a distinctly bulbous base up to 5cm/2in across which stains a reddy orange-brown if damaged or cut. The mushroom is rarely deeply rooted to its substrate and it differs

Above: The form shown here is the typical woodland type with dull brown colours. In gardens a larger white form with very bulbous stem base can be found.

Below: Very young caps can be quite hard to interpret as they look so different to mature mushrooms, but the early cracking of the cap is distinctive.

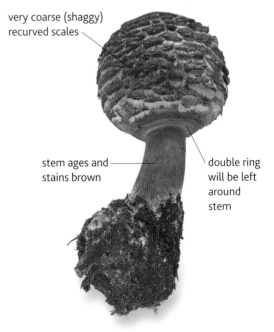

very coarse (shaggy) recurved scales

stem ages and stains brown

double ring will be left around stem

from the larger parasol which has a snakeskin pattern over the stem. Its smell is neutral. The spore print is whitish-cream.

HABITAT AND SEASON
Grows in woods and shrubberies, often with conifers, under hedges, along grassy roadsides, and even in parks. Relatively common, the season is early summer to late autumn.

STORAGE
It dries extremely well. Discard the stalk, cut the cap into sections and dry. Reconstituted, it is excellent in soups and casseroles.

PREPARATION AND COOKING HINTS
A clean cap needs little attention other than a light brushing. Discard the stalk and cut the cap into segments, then deep-fry or add to your soup or stew. Smaller caps are good for stuffing.

Below: The stems may be deep in leaf cover so look out for the bulbous base, which is a characteristic feature.

WARNING LOOKALIKE
One group of mushrooms that shaggy parasols could be mistaken for are dapperlings (*Lepiota* and *Echinoderma*, pages 138–39). Most are small and fragile with delicate scaly caps, free gills, both with and without a ring. However, some species, particularly *Echinoderma asperum* (pictured below), are large and with scales on the cap.

PARASOL
Macrolepiota procera

The parasol mushroom can grow quite large and has a long growing season. It reappears in the same place year after year, and may well have several fruitings during the season. The name is appropriate, as this mushroom does indeed look like a lady's parasol. The similar-looking shaggy parasol (see page 46) used to be considered a close relative.

IDENTIFICATION
The large cap, which is 12–28cm/4¼–11in or more, is spherical to begin with, but soon flattens out, though retaining a prominent centre. It is pale buff in colour and covered with symmetrical patterns of dark shaggy scales. The stem is 10–40cm/4–16in long and 1–2cm/½–¾in wide with speckled bands of cap colour on a white background, with a clavate to bulbous base. It also has a large double ring with cream upper and brown underside, which can slide up and down the stem, an important feature to help distinguish it from the dangerous dapperlings *Lepiota* spp. (see pages 138–39). The gills are free, remote from the stem, crowded, white to cream with brownish stains and a white edge, becoming darker in age but never turning green. The flesh is thin and white and has a fairly sweet mild milky smell. The spore print is white-cream to pinkish. This mushroom is best collected when dry as it soon absorbs moisture, becoming unpleasantly soggy.

HABITAT AND SEASON
In open areas of woods and pastures, and along roadside hedges. The season is from early summer to late autumn.

immovable scales on cap

large often double ring that can slide up and down the stem

slender stem growing from bulbous base

Above: Starting out concave and closed (known as 'drumstick'), the cap opens and flattens out as it grows.

Right: Note the coarse brown scales on the cap, the white ring and bands of brown scales on the stem.

STORAGE

This mushroom dries well. Discard the stems, which are tough, cut the cap into segments and dry. It reconsitutes well, and makes an excellent addition to soups and stews.

PREPARATION AND COOKING HINTS

The parasol makes for good eating, though it can disagree with some people so try out a little first. This mushroom is usually clean and maggot-free, however, you should dust off any particles on the top. Remove the stalk right into the cap and cut it into segments. The stalk is tougher, but edible. The parasol is good stuffed, battered and deep-fried, and dusted with seasoned flour and fried.

ANISEED TOADSTOOL
Clitocybe odora

The aniseed toadstool is most useful as a condiment. Be careful when you identify it, because verdigris roundhead, *Stropharia aeruginosa*, looks rather similar, although it has a blunt knob at the centre when open, and is always sticky and darkish green in colour. As the name suggests, aniseed toadstool has a very pungent aniseed smell.

IDENTIFICATION
The smooth, dry cap is 2–9cm/¾–3½in across. Convex at first, it soon flattens and can become wavy. The colour is pale greyish blue to greyish green, not or indistinctly hygrophanous, which darkens with age. The stem is 3–6cm/1¼–2½in long and 0.4–1.2cm/¼–½in wide, and has a frosted hoary base. The decurrent gills, which are the same colour as the cap, are close and run down the stem. The pale flesh smells strongly of aniseed. The spore print is pale pinkish-cream.

cap surface is dry, not sticky

greyish cap with tinge of blue green

gills are pale greenish-white

no ring on stem

WARNING LOOKALIKE
The *Stropharia aeruginosa* has a sticky cap and a ring on the (thinner) stem. It has no odour. The gills turn purple-brown when mature.

Above: The cap colour may fade rapidly from that shown to almost white. For safety, the paler specimens are best avoided in case of any confusion with the suspect fragrant funnel, *Clitocybe fragrans*, which is smaller, white and with a similar but more complex smell of aniseed and almonds.

HABITAT AND SEASON
Relatively common, these are found in leaf mould along the edges of coniferous and deciduous woods. In the latter they are likely to be in association with beech or sweet chestnut. The season is from late summer to late autumn.

STORAGE
Best dried and stored separately because of the intensity of its flavour and smell.

PREPARATION AND COOKING HINTS
It has a strong scent (hence the name) and is probably best used as a flavouring: finely chop fresh specimens or grind dried mushrooms to a powder and use as a seasoning.

THE MILLER
Another common funnel you might come across in the woods, with some superficial similarities to aniseed toadstool, is *Clitopilus prunulus* (the miller). White and wavy with thin decurrent cream gills, which turn pink as the spores mature, it in turn has a lookalike to avoid, fool's funnel. The miller is edible, but many prefer to avoid it due to risk of misidentification with poisonous funnels.

VELVET SHANK
Flammulina velutipes

As the name implies, velvet shank has a dark velvety stem. It normally grows during the winter months and can survive the frosts, indeed it may need a frost before starting to grow. It can be frozen solid, but still survive. This species is widely cultivated in Asia, although the commercial mushroom looks quite different to the wild; grown in glass jars, it forms dense clusters of tall thin white mushrooms.

IDENTIFICATION
The cap is 1–6cm/½–2½in across and fairly flat. It is light orange in colour, paler at the edges and darker towards the centre. It is also quite smooth and shiny with a sticky surface. The stem is

Above: Velvet shank is one of few mushrooms to be found over the winter months.

black, velvety
stem base

no ring
on stem

dense clusters
of stems

Above: Velvet shank is a saprotroph, often fruiting in abundance on large-diameter broadleaved deadwood. The caps can become quite viscid.

1–8cm/½–3in long and 0.2–1cm/up to ½in wide, very tough and is, as the name suggests, velvety and dark in colour, particularly at the base. The flesh, which is yellow on the cap changing to dark brown on the stem, has little smell. The gills are pale yellow. The spore print is creamy white.

HABITAT AND SEASON
Velvet shank often grows in very large clusters on dead or decaying wood, particularly in association with elm and oak. The season is long because they grow all through the winter months in more temperate zones and so are useful when only a limited number of mushrooms is available.

STORAGE
You can pickle them but probably the best method of storage is to dry and powder them.

PREPARATION AND COOKING HINTS
As they have a fairly tough texture these are best dried. If using fresh, cut off most of the stem, and slice the caps finely. They give a good flavour to soups and stews, but cook them well.

WARNING LOOKALIKES
Velvet shank is less likely to be confused with anything else because of its unusual season of growth, but it has similarities to the funeral bell (page 145) and, especially, sulphur tuft *Hypholoma fasciculare* (page 151). The spore print is different, also note the absence of a ring; the poisonous lookalikes will have a ring or a veil.

WAXCAPS
Hygrocybe species

There are approximately 60 species of waxcap known in northern Europe. The group has now been split after recent molecular work and the genus name *Hygrocybe* has been retained for only a few species. Some species have now be returned to the group *Cuphophyllus* from which they were formerly known and several other new genera have been recognised. They are, however, still collectively referred to as waxcaps.

Many waxcaps are quite common, although a few are endangered so should be avoided. They come up later in the autumn and into winter and prefer old undisturbed grassland and mossy soils. Meadow waxcap, *Cuphophyllus pratensis,* is considered the best edible species but snowy waxcap, *Cuphophyllus virgineus,* scarlet waxcap, *Hygrocybe coccinea,* and crimson waxcap, *Hygrocybe punicea,* are all worth collecting.

The waxcaps are often brightly coloured in shades of yellow, orange and red but white, grey, green, pink and brown species also exist. Many look very similar to one another, are hard to tell apart and can be a difficult group to identify. Some are considered toxic. The group is

separated by several important field characters: firstly, whether stems and caps are dry, moist or viscid; next, colour; and finally, gill attachment. All waxcaps have white spore prints.

MEADOW WAXCAP *Cuphophyllus pratensis*
Meadow waxcaps are stout, medium to large mushrooms (cap 2–10cm/¾–4in) with dry white/cream stems (3–15cm x 0.5–2cm/1¼–6in x ¼–¾in), dry pale orange caps and strongly decurrent buff/cream gills. It tastes mild and without a distinct smell. Meadow waxcap occurs solitary or in groups from July through to November (January) in grasslands, lawns, fixed dunes and occasionally in woodland and woodland pasture. A smaller pale variety, appropriately named pale waxcap, *Cuphophyllus pratensis* var. *pallida* is similar except for the white colours and could be confused with the poisonous fool's funnel, *Clitocybe rivulosa*.

SNOWY WAXCAP *Cuphophyllus virgineus*
Snowy waxcap is a small to medium species (cap 1–7cm/under ½–2¾in) with a white,

Below: Meadow waxcap (*Cuphophyllus pratensis*) has a pale orange cap with cream stem, often found in rings.

Below: Snowy waxcap (*Cuphophyllus virgineus*) is tiny and white (beware fool's funnel and destroying angel).

Above: Scarlet waxcap (*H. Coccinea*) is small with a convex cap, a yellowy-orange stem and scarlet cap.

Above: The less-common crimson waxcap (*H. Punicea*) is similar of course to the scarlet, but is larger.

moist and slippery, hygrophanous cap. It has a smooth dry white stem (2–6cm x 0.2–1cm/¾–2½in x under ½in) and decurrent white gills. There is no distinctive taste or smell. One of the most common waxcaps, it is found growing solitary or in groups from August to November (January) in unimproved grassland, lawns, scrub, road verges and occasionally in woodland. Another similar-looking waxcap but with slightly buffer colours is cedarwood waxcap *Cuphophyllus russociaceus,* which has a very characteristic strong smell of Russian leather! This is considered not edible.

SCARLET WAXCAP *Hygrocybe coccinea*
This is a medium sized waxcap (cap 1–6cm/ under ½–2½in) with a scarlet to orange, slightly greasy, convex cap. With a hand lens one can see that the cap surface is finely veined or knobbly. The stem (2–7cm x 0.3–0.6cm/¾–2¾in x under ¼in) is always smooth, dry and matt with similar colours to the cap or paler with a little yellow. The gills are adnate, occasionally with a decurrent tooth and can be reddish with a yellow edge or entirely yellow. Smell and taste neutral. It occurs in groups from July to December in unimproved grassland, lawns, fixed dunes, and deciduous woodland.

The shape and colours of this mushroom can be extremely variable. It can be confused with the much larger crimson waxcap, *Hygrocybe punicea* (see below) and splendid waxcap, *Hygrocybe splendidissima*. However, the former has a more viscid cap and the latter an entirely dry cap (and smells of honey as it dries); they both also have narrowly adnate gills, unlike the broad attachment in *H. coccinea*.

CRIMSON WAXCAP *Hygrocybe punicea*
Normally the largest waxcap one is likely to encounter, crimson waxcap has a dark red, slippery viscid cap (3–15cm/1¼–6in) which is initially broadly conical becoming flattened with age. The stem is dry and fibrous (2–15cm x 0.5–1.3cm/¾–3in) with red, orange and yellow tones tapering to a white base. The gills are thick and rather distant, narrowly adnate to emarginate with a decurrent tooth. The gill colour is quite variable, with cinnamon, red and purple tones with a yellow edge. There is neither a distinctive smell nor taste to the crimson waxcap. The mushroom is typically found from August to December growing in unimproved grassland and scrub, and its presence is generally a good indicator of high conservation-value grasslands.

AMETHYST DECEIVER
Laccaria amethystina

Amethyst deceivers can grow in large groups. They are colourful, edible and tasty. However, it is now known that these mushrooms accumulate toxins from the surrounding environment such as arsenic and hydrogen cyanide. So use sparingly and only occasionally.

IDENTIFICATION
The cap is 1–4cm/½–1½in across. It is convex but flattens with age and develops a slight depression in the centre. Deep purplish lilac in colour, it dries to an almost buff colour. The stem is 3–8cm/1¼–3in long and 0.3–0.7cm/

Above: When picked, amethyst deceivers are bright in colour, but this will fade.

cap becomes much paler when dry

broadly spaced gills

under ¼in wide, hollow and with slightly white fibres below the cap. The gills are widely spaced, adnate to shortly decurrent, and similar colour to the cap. The flesh is thin and tinged lilac. The smell is not distinctive. The spore print is white.

HABITAT AND SEASON
Grows in deciduous woods, often with beech, chestnut, oak, birch and hazel. The season is late summer to early winter. It is very common.

STORAGE
Excellent fresh, they also dry very well. They can also be blanched and stored in spiced alcohol to give a most unusual dessert sauce (keep in the refrigerator).

PREPARATION AND COOKING HINTS
As these sometimes grow quite densely and have wide open gills, they can be dirty, so it is important to clean them well before using.

DECEIVER
Laccaria laccata

As the name suggests, this fungus has many lookalikes and is less distinct than amethyst deceivers, but like its relative it can grow in large groups. Its habitat and season are the same, as are the suggestions for storage and preparation. The deceiver is incredibly variable and it may take you a number of seasons to recognise the many variations.

The deceiver has a cap similar in size to the amethyst deceiver, 1–4cm/½–1½in, but is also convex and flattening. It can open to look like an autumn chanterelle. The colour is tawny to pale red and it dries to a paler colour. The stem is 2–7cm/¾–2¾in long and 0.2–0.5cm/under ¼in wide, a similar colour to the cap, but often twisted. The gills are adnate to shortly decurrent, and widely spaced. The flesh is a pale reddish-brown and the smell is not distinctive. The spore print is white.

Above: Widely spaced gills, cinnamon to buff in colour.

thin tough stem

cap margin can be wavy

widely-spaced light brown gills

WARNING LOOKALIKES
Both deceivers can be deceived in turn by *Inocybe geophylla* (white fibrecap) and the var. *lilacina* (lilac fibrecap), which has a distinctive purple rounded cap that can look similar to the amethyst particularly in the early stages of growth. They have a milky coffee-brown spore print, however.

FAIRY RING CHAMPIGNON
Marasmius oreades

Left: One of the earliest mushrooms to appear, the fairy ring champignon is a delight for the forager.

This enchanting mushroom goes by a few other names, including mousserons, scotch bonnet, and fairy ring fungus. One of the first mushrooms to appear in spring, fairy ring champignon tastes just as good as it looks. But beware, there is a poisonous lookalike, *Clitocybe rivulosa*, that grows in a very similar way. There is very little similarity once they are fully grown, but it is important not to make mistakes. The fairy mushroom must always be cooked.

IDENTIFICATION
The cap is 1–5cm/½–2in across, convex at first, then flattening with quite a marked centre. Tan in colour, it dries to a fairly light buff. The stem is 4–8cm/1½–3in long and 0.3–0.6cm/under ¼in wide, minutely hairy, but tough, so it is best to remove the stem entirely and just eat the cap. The gills are white to tan and quite distant. There is sometimes a bitter almond scent. The flesh is thick. The spore print is white.

HABITAT AND SEASON
This mushroom forms rings in the shorter grass of old pastures or lawns. The season is from late spring to late autumn. It is very common (if perhaps unpopular with some gardeners who find it on their lawns).

STORAGE
These mushrooms are wonderful cooked and eaten fresh, but they dry very well. They can also be blanched and stored in red Vermouth, olive oil, or wine or cider vinegar.

Above: *Marasmius oreades*. Dark rings in grassland are a good indication of where to look for these mushrooms.

Above: This classic fairy ring is a few metres across, but they can reach more than a hundred metres!

PREPARATION AND COOKING HINTS

As long as you pick these mushrooms clean and cut off the stems, the only problem you are likely to have is removing a few blades of grass. Occasionally a light dusting with a brush may be necessary, but washing spoils the flavour. It has an oaky scent when cooked, and is lovely just in sweet butter. From a culinary point of view this is a very versatile mushroom.

WARNING LOOKALIKE

It is important to be able to distinguish between this mushroom and *Clitocybe rivulosa* or fool's funnel (see page 136). This species also grows in rings, often very close to those of the fairy ring champignon. The colour and gills are different, and *C. rivulosa* does not appear so early in the year, but it is essential that you can identify it.

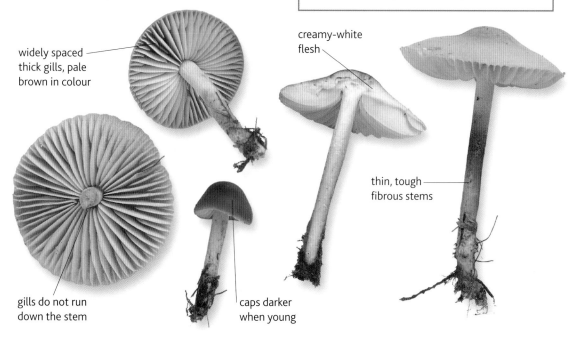

widely spaced thick gills, pale brown in colour

gills do not run down the stem

caps darker when young

creamy-white flesh

thin, tough fibrous stems

BRANCHING OYSTER
Pleurotus cornucopiae

This member of the oyster mushroom family is fairly widely spread. It can be found on the same trees and at the same time as the oyster mushroom, so always have a good look for it before you leave the tree.

IDENTIFICATION
The cap is 2–15cm/¾–6in across and convex. It often makes quite a funnel-like shape, which frequently becomes fluted and split at the edges. Pale yellowish to grey brown when young, it turns a fairly dark brown with age. The stem is 3–11cm/1¼–4¼ long and 0.7–2cm/¼–¾in wide. Several fans may grow from the same stem, rather like flowers. The gills are are deeply decurrent and run down the stem, forming anatomising ridges right to the stem base; they are white to light tan in colour. The flesh is white and has a rather sweet aniseed smell which turns mealy when cut. The spore print is white to lilac.

HABITAT AND SEASON
This mushroom grows in dense clusters on cut stumps and fallen trunks of most deciduous trees, in particular dead elm, oak and beech. The season is spring to late autumn.

Above: Strongly decurrent gills continue all the way to the base of the stem forming a 'network' of fine ridges.

STORAGE
It can be maggoty so pick with care. This mushroom air-dries well.

PREPARATION AND COOKING HINTS
If picked carefully, only a light wipe should be necessary. Discard most of the stalk as it will be quite tough, particularly where it was attached to the tree. The pleasant, coconut-like flavour makes it good in mixed mushroom dishes.

Above: The light gills of the branching oyster anastomose down the stem in a crisscrossing pattern.

often deep funnel-like cap

OYSTER MUSHROOM
Pleurotus ostreatus

Now grown commercially on a fairly large scale and so quite familiar, it is still exciting to find a wild oyster mushroom. They grow on dead or decaying trees, often in large masses. They will grow in the same place in successive years, so remember where you picked them. Oyster mushrooms grow in groups, one on top of the other, and if carefully removed from the tree are usually very clean.

IDENTIFICATION
The cap is 5–15cm/2–6in across. It is shaped rather like a fan and larger specimens may have fluted edges. The colour can vary: usually a slate grey, they can sometimes have a brown or bluish tinge. They have almost no stem. The decurrent gills run down the stem; cream to pale grey at first, they can become more brown with age. The flesh is white with a mushroomy smell. The spore print is white to lilac grey.

HABITAT AND SEASON
These occur in large clusters on standing trees or on the stumps of fallen trees. Most commonly found on beech trees, they will grow on other trees, especially elm. The season is all year round.

Above: This is the grey-brown late-autumn/winter *Pleurotus ostreatus*. In summer, the cream-coloured pale oyster, *P. pulmonarius* (below), is more common.

STORAGE
All methods of storage can be used. If you separate the caps they air-dry very successfully.

PREPARATION AND COOKING HINTS
If picked carefully they are likely to be clean and a wipe with a damp cloth is probably all they need. The oyster is extremely versatile and works well in all kinds of dishes.

crowded gills run down the stem

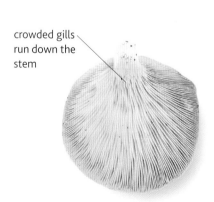

stems may be absent

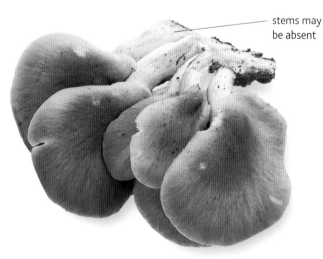

SAFFRON MILKCAP
Lactarius deliciosus

A lovely, colourful mushroom to find, this grows under pine on neutral and calcareous soils., which can make cleaning difficult. It also has a hollow stem which can lead to problems with infestation. To avoid this problem just pick young fresh specimens, but at the same time make sure that they are mature enough for a positive identification, otherwise they can be confused with the poisonous woolly milkcaps.

IDENTIFICATION
The cap is 4–11cm/1½–4¼in across, convex with a depressed centre. It has concentric rings and, as the name suggests, is saffron in colour; it is usually a brighter orange than its lookalikes. On cutting, you will notice that it bleeds a carrot-coloured milk. It also has a clean, inrolled edge (this is an important means of identification, because neither the woolly milkcap nor *L. pubescens* have clean edges to the cap, and have a spicy-tasting white rather than carroty-tasting orange milk). The orange gills

Above: The cap becomes pale, almost silvery-white or dull greenish with age. Pick the fresher orange caps.

are crowded, and adnate to slightly decurrent. The hollow stem is 3–9cm/1¾–3½in long and 1–2cm/½–¾in wide, slightly paler than the cap but always pockmarked with orange, and when bruised, turning slightly greenish. The flesh is pale. The spore print is white.

OAK AND OTHER MILKCAPS
There are many species of edible (and poisonous) milkcap. *Lactarius quietus* or oak milkcap, also considered edible, has a duller pale orange cap and stem, with cream to cinnamon gills; it exudes a white rather than orange milk. It is found under oaks rather than pines, but be wary of confusing it with the inedible but mild milkcap, *L. helvus*.

Left: The cap margin is inrolled in young orange specimens.

Above: *Lactarius deliciosus* grows under pine with a pitted stem and zonate cap.

HABITAT AND SEASON
Always grows under pine trees (hence its other name of red pine mushroom), and can also be found beside paths on sandy terrain. The season is early summer to quite late autumn. It is relatively common.

STORAGE
This stores extremely well, whether dried or in oil or vinegar.

PREPARATION AND COOKING HINTS
The sand and pine needles of this mushroom's habitat make cleaning important. It may be necessary to wash your specimens immediately before cooking, but then dry them well before slicing and cooking them. The lovely firm crunchy texture and good (if mild) flavour make this a much sought-after mushroom.

WARNING LOOKALIKES
There are a few similar but poisonous species to look out for: *Lactarius pubescens* and *L. torminosus* (see page 140) and false saffron milkcap (*L. deterrimus*), below, which is considered edible but not sought after. It is found under spruce not pine, and exudes an orange milk that gradually turns red. The cap is often flushed with green.

CHARCOAL BURNER
Russula cyanoxantha

Charcoal burner is an excellent mushroom to eat. However, it is a member of a large genus and identification within the group can be very difficult. There are other brittlegills that are edible; the powdery (*R. parazurea*) and greencracked (*R. virescens*) also have varied-coloured dull green to grey caps. Correct identification is essential because some *Russula* are poisonous, in particular the beechwood sickener, *Russula nobilis* and the sickener, *R. emetica*. As always, if in doubt leave it out.

Above: Showing the range of outfits, this charcoal burner has a green tinge to its concave cap.

IDENTIFICATION
The cap is 5–15cm/2–6in across and slightly greasy. Convex at first, it opens out with a shallow depression in the centre. Occasionally a single colour but more often than not quite a mixed shade, ranging from purple to light green, frequently with a rather faded appearance. The stem is 5–10cm/2–4in long and 1.5–3cm/½–

cap is often of mixed colours or even green

firm stem is white, sometimes flushed lavender

crowded white gills

Above: The dull violet-purple cap shown here is typical, but beware, the cap is often mixed with green. The best means of identification is to brush your fingers over the gills, as they should feel flexible and not crumbly as most other *Russulas* are.

1¼in wide, and white. The gills are pure white. An identification feature of the charcoal burner is that the gills do not break away if they are touched; they are soft and flexible, and quite clearly joined to the cap margin. This is in marked contrast to some *Russula* species that

Right: A large and colourful group of *Russula* species. The mushrooms in this family are some of the most difficult to identify accurately.

WARNING LOOKALIKES
There are many similar-looking *Russulas* to be wary of, which if not deadly, are harmful to eat, such as the bright red sickeners *R. emetica* and *R. nobilis* (see page 141). The charcoal burner is one of the few brittlegills with gills that aren't, in fact, brittle.

have crumbly, brittle gills. The flesh is white and the smell is pleasant. The spore print is pure white. It is most likely to be mistaken for *Russula grisea*, which is also edible but has a cream spore print and crumbly gills.

HABITAT AND SEASON
Usually to be found under broad-leaved trees., particularly oak and beech. The season is summer to late autumn and it can be very common.

STORAGE
Drying is a very good method of storing the charcoal burner.

PREPARATION AND COOKING HINTS
It is rare to find a perfect specimen, as woodland wildlife attack it from almost the moment it appears. As a result it will need careful cleaning. However, it is good fresh or dried, with a mild nutty flavour, and will add an interesting taste and texture to your mushroom dishes, as it retains its crunchiness when cooked.

WOOD BLEWIT
Lepista nuda

The wood blewit is a rich and flowery-smelling mushroom that is useful because it appears late in the season. But beware – some people are allergic to it. Make sure you try only a little first and take care if you serve it to guests. It must be well-cooked and never eaten raw.

IDENTIFICATION
The cap is 5–15cm/2–6in across. Convex at first, it eventually flattens and is sometimes quite irregular. The cap starts by being quite blue but then turns an almost shiny tan. It dries a little paler. The stem is 5–9cm/2–3½in long and 1–2.5cm/½–1in wide, and often has purple markings. The gills are adnate to emarginate, crowded, and very lilac; although they lose their colour with age they never turn brown. It is best to pick younger specimens that still retain the wonderful colour, for these have the best flavour. The flesh is bluish and the smell is quite perfumed; some describe it like frozen orange juice. The spore print is a pale pink.

HABITAT AND SEASON
Grows in all mixed woodland, hedges and gardens and sometimes on open ground. The season is from autumn to early winter. It is quite common and often grows in large quantities. *Lepista sordida* is similar but less robust and can be found from early summer.

gills remain violet, never turn brown

smooth, often slippery cap surface

tough, fibrous stem

soil matter often attached when picked

Right: Although these specimens are under pines, the blewit is equally common in deciduous woods and gardens.

Below: Note that the caps are smooth and not sticky. The gills remain violet, never turning rusty brown as do those of some lookalike species, such as *Cortinarius*.

but as it has a very pronounced taste it goes particularly well with strongly flavoured vegetables such as onions and leeks. It must always be well-cooked, and do not forget that some people are allergic to it, so test first.

STORAGE
Because the wood blewit must be cooked before it is eaten, it is best not to dry it. It does, however, keep extremely well if it is blanched and then put in wine vinegar, extra-virgin olive oil or spiced alcohol. But, if kept in the alcohol, store in the refrigerator to stop fermentation.

PREPARATION AND COOKING HINTS
Quite an easy mushroom to clean, gently wipe the top and cut the stem. The colour and fragrance mean it can be used in both sweet and savoury dishes. It is good in all mushroom dishes,

WARNING LOOKALIKES
Be careful not to confuse the wood blewit with a webcap, in particular *Cortinarius purpurascens*. This is not itself poisonous, but all webcaps are best avoided. They have a rusty-brown spore print.

FIELD BLEWIT
Lepista personata

Previously known as *Lepista saeva*, field blewit is most commonly found exactly where the name suggests. But, because they are low-growing, they are difficult to spot in long grass. Its other name, blue leg or pied bleu, comes from the brightly coloured stem. Like the wood blewit, field blewit has a strong, woody flavour. It is best picked when young, to avoid infestation with maggots. Blewits are satrotrophic fungi, so are often very well attached to the soil or leaf litter they are growing in. Remember, like wood blewit, this mushroom must be cooked before it is eaten and some people are allergic to it, so take particular care.

IDENTIFICATION
The cap is 5–20cm/2–8in across. Quite convex at first, then flattening, it can be slightly depressed when fully opened out. The cap is a rather insignificant buff colour, but it has a nice shine, and a slightly damp feel. The stem, which is 3–7cm/1¼–2¾in long and 1.5–3cm/½–1¼in wide, is the most significant thing about the field blewit. It is often rather bulbous and has lilac markings. The flesh is quite thick and chunky, and white to buff-coloured. The gills are emarginate to adnate, crowded and whitish. It has a perfumed smell very similar to that of the wood blewit. The spore print is pale pink.

these are in perfect condition for picking

pale and fibrous interior

no violet in gills

bluish-lilac stem may fade when old

HABITAT AND SEASON
Often grows in large numbers in rings in pasture. The season is autumn through to the first frosts, although it can stand light frosts.

STORAGE
As this is another mushroom that must be cooked before it is eaten, it is best blanched and stored in wine vinegar or extra-virgin olive oil, or in spiced alcohol to serve with a dessert.

PREPARATION AND COOKING HINTS
This must always be cooked. Very similar to wood blewit, field blewit gives a really good flavour to stews if it is chopped up first.

Right: Here, you can see clearly the complete lack of violet colour in the cap, compared to wood blewit.

OTHER BLEWITS AND LOOKALIKES
There are other edible blewits you might come across, such as *Lepista panaeola* (previously *L. luscina*), below left, and the more common *Lepista sordida* (below right), which can appear similar respectively to the wood and field blewits. In terms of warning lookalikes, field blewit is relatively straightforward to identify correctly, with its distinctive lilac stem contrasting with the light-coloured cap and gills, but there is some risk of misidentifying the lilac-capped blewits (including the *Lepista sordida*) with *Cortinarius purpurascens,* bruising webcap (see page 67) or *Cortinarius violaceus*, violet webcap.

HORSE MUSHROOM
Agaricus arvensis

This is one of the larger varieties of mushroom. It is quite meaty in texture and has a very distinctive aniseed or almond smell. Horse mushrooms are best picked when they are young because not only are they soon attacked by maggots, but also the flesh becomes dark brown with age and will turn any cooked dish muddy brown.

Horse mushrooms prefer open meadows or woodland edges. These mushrooms tend to come up in the same places year after year, so having once found a good growth keep watching in future years.

Horse mushrooms vary in colour from white to cream but often have yellowish markings on the cap.; starting out as white, they age to a dull brassy yellow. When you find one like this,

> **AGARICUS**
> Listed on the following pages in order of Latin name, not popularity, members of the *Agaricus* family do look similar. They also change quite dramatically as they mature. White when young, they open and flatten, and the colour of the gills can develop from pale pink to dark brown. Some caps are smooth, some scaly, or yellow.

check it particularly carefully to ensure that it is not, in fact, a yellow stainer, *Agaricus xanthodermus*, which can make some people very ill if they eat it. Unlike yellow stainers, however, the insides of horse mushrooms do not stain golden yellow when scratched or cut.

cap is usually smooth but can sometimes be slightly scaly and yellow when older

light at first, the mature gills turn dark brown

ring still attached to cap margin; the ring will develop cogwheel-like markings on its underside

Above: A young horse mushroom appears tight and white, opening and changing colour as it matures.

Above: It has an expanded creamy flat cap when mature.

STORAGE
These mushrooms dry well, but it is important to check thoroughly that they are insect free. Slice and then dry in an open or electric drier.

PREPARATION AND COOKING HINTS
These mushrooms make wonderful meals, provided, of course, that they are not maggoty. Remember, too, if you are using older specimens when the flesh has turned dark brown, that they will change the colour of your cooked dish.

IDENTIFICATION
The cap can be from 6–15cm/2½–6in across. It is domed at first, but eventually expands to a fully convex shape. It is white but yellows with age, and can be smooth or scaly. The stem can be 5.5–12cm/2¼–4½in long and 1–2.2cm/½–¾in wide, and has a membranous ring with cogwheel-like scales on the underside. The gills are free and whitish at first, then turn a delicate pink and eventually dark brown in mature specimens. The flesh is thick and white but darkens with age and can become a little woolly lower down the stem. It has a distinct smell of aniseed or almonds. The spore print is dark chocolate brown.

The mature macro mushroom (page 78) can appear similar, but grows to a larger size.

HABITAT AND SEASON
Horse mushrooms are quite common everywhere in open woodland, parks and meadows. Their season is from midsummer (sometimes earlier) to late autumn and they often grow in large rings.

WARNING LOOKALIKE
Yellow stainers (see page 148) from the same *Agaricus* family are commonly mistaken for horse (or field or wood) mushrooms. Their most distinctive feature is that the flesh turns yellow when touched or cut, though this can fade, and they have a strong, acrid, almost carbolic smell.

THE PRINCE
Agaricus augustus

The prince is a relatively uncommon but good mushroom to find: not only does it look attractive, but it also has a lovely flavour and tastes delicious. These mushrooms tend to grow in deciduous and coniferous woodland, and in small groups rather than rings.

IDENTIFICATION
The cap is 7–22cm/2¾–8½in across – or larger. Button-shaped at first, it opens to a convex form and is often irregular in shape. It is cream to light brown in colour and has clearly marked rings of yellowish-tawny to reddish-brown fibrous scales. The stem is 8–20cm/3–8in long and 1.5–2.5cm/½–1in wide, often club-shaped, off-white with small scales below a large, fragile floppy ring. The gills are free, off-white at first, turning dark brown with age. The flesh is thick, white turning slowly yellow to pink, and smells pleasant like aniseed or almonds. The spore print is dark chocolate brown.

cap surface always has flattened scales

large floppy ring

the stem is usually fibrous or scaly

Above: The prince is usually found at the edges of woods, clearings or pathsides, rarely very far from trees.

HABITAT AND SEASON
The prince grows mainly in coniferous and deciduous woods, sometimes parkland, often found in groups. The season is late summer to late autumn.

STORAGE
As these mushrooms grow fairly large, make sure you have good specimens before slicing and drying them in the usual way. This is a good mushroom to store for winter use as it has an intensity of flavour that will enhance any mushroom dish.

PREPARATION AND COOKING HINTS
A nice mushroom that needs very little preparation. The stem tends to be quite fibrous, so is best discarded. The cap does not need peeling, just wipe lightly with a damp cloth before slicing. The prince makes an extremely good addition to omelettes, but is also excellent on its own.

CULTIVATED MUSHROOM
Agaricus bisporus

Agaricus bisporus is very similar in smell and taste to the field mushroom. It is believed to be the species from which most of the cultivated varieties come, and so is included here. It can grow in quite large quantities and is mostly found in urban habitats and on waste ground.

IDENTIFICATION
The cap is 5–12cm/2–4½in across, button-shaped before opening almost flat. It is whitish to mid-brown with flaky scales.The stem is 3.5–8cm/1½–3in long and 1–2.5cm/½–1in wide, and white, with a distinct ring below the cap. It has pink gills which are free and become darker with age. The flesh is white, bruising slightly reddish, and has a distinct mushroomy smell. The spore print is dark chocolate brown.

HABITAT AND SEASON
It grows on compost heaps, in garden waste and beside roads, occasionally on the edges of hedges and small plantations, but very rarely in grass. The season is summer to autumn. It is quite common.

STORAGE
This mushroom tends to be quite small and dries well, either whole or cut.

PREPARATION AND COOKING HINTS
Because this mushroom often grows on compost heaps or in rough ground, it is best to wipe the cap very thoroughly, cutting off the bottom of the stem and slicing through. It is full of flavour.

Above and right: *Agaricus bisporus* is the species that cultivated varieties come from. The widely available button (white), cup and flat mushrooms are the different stages of growth of this mushroom.

FIELD MUSHROOM
Agaricus campestris

The field mushroom is probably the best known of all wild mushrooms. Years ago fields were often carpeted with these small white mushrooms, but due to changes in farming technology and the greater use of herbicides, pesticides and, particularly, nitrates, many of the natural pastures where field mushrooms grew have disappeared. If you are lucky enough to have some old meadows and horse-grazed pasture near you, keep an eye open for a wonderful feast that can come up at any time from quite early in the summer through to autumn. These mushrooms are best picked early in the morning, not only to beat other mushroom collectors, but also to ensure that they have not yet been attacked by maggots, which love them too.

IDENTIFICATION
The cap is 4–10cm/1½–4in across. It retains its dome shape for some time before opening out fully. It is silky white, ageing to a light brown. The stem is 2.5–8.5cm/1–3¼in long and

Above: *Agaricus campestris* can vary widely in appearance; some have scaly or fibrous brown and cream caps, as here.

ring is fragile and often missing

gills are pink when young, then brown

Above: Note that the gills are free and not attached to the stem; this feature is common to all *Agaricus*.

Above: The silky cap of the *Agaricus campestris* typically overhangs slightly at the edges.

0.8–2cm/¼–¾in wide, tapering to the base, and has a thin ring which is often torn away. Even in unopened field mushrooms the gills are free, and deep pink, a useful identification feature. The white flesh bruises slightly pink and has a pleasant smell. The spore print is dark brown.

HABITAT AND SEASON
Field mushrooms grow in lawns, meadows, open grassland and mature pasture. They can grow any time from early summer through to late autumn. They often grow in rings.

STORAGE
An excellent mushroom for storing dried as it retains its flavour extremely well. Smaller specimens can be threaded on string and dried whole, but larger ones should be sliced.

PREPARATION AND COOKING HINTS
These do not need peeling, a wipe with a damp cloth is sufficient, but do check them carefully to make sure there is no maggot infestation. The best way to do this is to trim the stem carefully and slice through the centre – any maggots will then be easy to see. The older specimens are best used for ketchup, sauces and stews, as these give a quite intense, dark brown colour to the dish. Young specimens can be used as you like. They are delicious on their own for breakfast.

WARNING LOOKALIKES
As with other *Agaricus*, in particular the horse and blushing wood, the most common mistake in identifying a field mushroom is picking a yellow stainer (see page 148). Deathcap (132) and destroying angel (134) are also ones to be wary of, as the immature button stages are similar.

BLUSHING WOOD MUSHROOM
Agaricus sylvaticus

This is a fairly common mushroom found mainly in coniferous and broadleaf woodland, never in open pasture, and grows in groups in the same places year after year.

IDENTIFICATION
The cap is 2.5–12cm/1–4½in across, convex, depressed at the centre and covered with brown scales which give it an overall broken pattern. The stem is 4.5–13cm/1¾–5¼in long and 0.8–2cm/½–¾in wide, with a swollen base; whitish, but striated with brown markings below a brown, sometimes double ring. The gills are free, greyish pink at first, then dark brown. The flesh is white and stains bright red when cut at the base or lengthwise. It has very little smell. The spore print is dark chocolate brown.

HABITAT AND SEASON
The usual habitat is coniferous and broadleaf woods and the season is from early summer to late autumn.

Above: This small mushroom typically has a thin stem with a bulbous base, which distinguishes it from the very similar *A. langei* (scaly wood mushroom).

STORAGE
The blushing wood is best dried, but as it is often large, it should be sliced first.

PREPARATION AND COOKING HINTS
This mushroom is excellent to eat, and has quite an intense flavour. Because it grows only in woodlands, the top will need to be brushed to remove any leaves or pine needles. Cut off and discard the lower portion of the stem, then slice. It will give a wonderful nutty flavour to your dishes. It is also good on its own, lightly sautéed with a little butter.

brown scaly
cap surface
scratches red

ring with small scale
on underside

WARNING LOOKALIKE
Blushing wood mushrooms could be confused with the yellow stainer (page 148) but unlike the latter, its flesh will stain red not yellow when bruised or cut.

WOOD MUSHROOM
Agaricus sylvicola

Wood mushrooms have many similarities to the horse mushroom but, as the name suggests, it only grows in woodland (despite its name, it is not closely related to the blushing wood).

IDENTIFICATION
The cap is 7–11cm/2¾–4¼in across, domed at first before opening out to be almost flat. It is a creamy white to yellow, darkening with age, and yellows when handled. The stem is 7–10cm/2¾–4in long and 0.7–1.5cm/¼–½in wide, often bulbous (sometimes abruptly so) with a thin broad hanging ring, and yellowish to whitish scales on the underside. The gills are free, white then pinkish grey before turning dark brown. The flesh is white and has an aniseed or almond smell. The spore print is dark chocolate brown.

HABITAT AND SEASON
Wood mushrooms are quite common in coniferous and deciduous woods, particularly oak and beech. Its season is summer to autumn.

WARNING LOOKALIKES
Take care not to confuse this one with either the yellow stainer (page 148), or some of the deadly *Amanitas*. It does not grow out of a volval cup, so there will be no sign of one, and if you turn the mushroom over or cut it you will quite clearly see its identifying features. If in any doubt, leave alone.

STORAGE
These mushrooms do not store well, so use and enjoy them as soon as possible after you have picked them.

PREPARATION AND COOKING HINTS
The young specimens are particularly tasty, similar to horse mushrooms with an aniseed flavour. Try coating the caps of young mushrooms in seasoned flour, then dipping them in a batter made with beer or sparkling water and deep-frying them: simply delicious.

Above and right: Always a graceful slender mushroom, wood mushrooms grow exclusively in woodlands.

MACRO MUSHROOM
Agaricus urinascens

Previously known as *Agaricus macrosporus*, this is quite a common autumn mushroom, similar to the horse mushroom but larger and scalier. It often grows in rings and is extremely good to eat.

IDENTIFICATION
The domed cap is usually 8–15cm/3–6in across, though can reach 30cm/12in. It is off-white with minute buff scales. The stem is 5–10cm/2–4in long and 2.5–5cm/1–2in wide, scaly below the broad floppy ring, which is coarsely scaly on the underside, off-white and quite thick, with a slightly pointed base. The gills are pale pink at

Above: This fungus can form huge rings of dinnerplate-sized mushrooms.

thick ring with scaly underside

gills free from the stem

first, turning darker brown with age. The flesh is white and has a fairly distinct smell of almonds or aniseed – older specimens can have a less pleasant aroma, as suggested by its Latin name. The spore print is mid to dark brown.

HABITAT AND SEASON
Grows in open woodland and mature pastures that have not been treated with chemicals. The season is autumn.

STORAGE
Check larger ones, as they may be maggoty. This mushroom is best dried if preserving, but specimens can be quite large so it is important to slice them first.

Above: The macro often has a thick stem and quite distinctive fine brown scales on the cap.

PREPARATION AND COOKING HINTS
Very good to eat. Clean the stem and brush the cap; peeling is usually unnecessary. The mushroom can turn your dish dark brown.

WARNING LOOKALIKE
Some care over identification is necessary, because macro mushroom can look like the poisonous yellow stainer (see page 148). However, the shape of the cap and, in particular, the smell are useful aids to ensuring you have the right mushroom.

SHAGGY INKCAP OR LAWYER'S WIG
Coprinus comatus

One of the most common mushrooms, these often come up in dense clusters on newly turned earth in meadows and gardens throughout the summer. Only the young specimens are edible and once picked they must be used quickly, otherwise they soon decay into a nasty inky mass. This is an easy mushroom to identify as it is very distinct, although care must be taken that the early stages of this and the magpie fungus, *Coprinopsis picacea*, are not mistaken. However, magpie inkcap has some veil-like patches covering the cap, while shaggy inkcap does not.

IDENTIFICATION
The cap is 2–7cm/¾–2¾in across and 4–15cm/1½–6in deep; egg-shaped at first, it opens out into a bell. White with a cream-coloured top or centre, it has large shaggy scales. The stem is 5–30cm/2–12in long and 1–2.5cm/½–1in wide, and white. The gills are tight and white to start with, slowly changing to black from the edge inwards before becoming a mass of ink which, incidentally, makes good drawing ink. There is a delicate and moveable, narrow ring that remains on the stem as the cap grows away. The flesh is white with a slight sweet smell. The spore print is black.

HABITAT AND SEASON
Widespread on grassy banks beside roads, on compost heaps, lawns and recently disturbed soil near building sites. The season is from midsummer to late autumn. They are very common. (In fact, shaggy inkcaps are more frequently spotted than common inkcaps, despite the latter's name.)

WARNING LOOKALIKES
A mushroom to avoid, especially in its younger stage of growth as it has a similar shape and patchy cap, is magpie inkcap *Coprinopsis picacea* (right). And there is also, of course, the common inkcap (see page 150), *Coprinopsis atramentaria*; although not poisonous by itself it isn't considered edible due to the extreme adverse effects if it is consumed with any alcohol. In appearance it is smoother, shorter and greyer, and so fairly easy to distinguish from the shaggy inkcap.

Above: This is the best stage to collect shaggy ink caps for cooking, when they are young and white.

cap scales
curled back

cap margin
liquifies to
release
spores

ring which
remains on
the stem

hollow stem

STORAGE
Best used quickly after picking. You can dry
them in an electric drier, but do not attempt to
air-dry them as they will turn into an inky mass.

PREPARATION AND COOKING HINTS
Although shaggy inkcaps can be used dried,
they are really best used fresh and when young
and white, and they don't keep well after
picking. Eat on their own, or combined with the
parasol mushroom, *Macrolepiota procera*,
perhaps with onions and potato in a soup.

Right: The distinct narrow ring is not always seen, but
as the cap expands it will be left behind on the stem.

CEP OR PENNY BUN
Boletus edulis

Also known as the porcini, mushroom hunters regard this mushroom as a great prize; it has a wonderful nutty flavour and is extremely versatile. It grows over a number of days and can grow very big and weigh as much as 1kg/2¼lb. However, if fungus gnats lay their eggs their larvae enter at the base of the stem and the maggots work their way up to the cap and tubes, so it is important to pick only those in prime condition. When collecting large specimens, cut

Below: A variable species – the caps are frequently quite pale brown and the stem can often be very swollen, but this is not always the case.

Above: Ceps are a culinary delicacy, considered at their best when small.

the cap in half to make sure there is no maggot infestation before putting it in your basket.

IDENTIFICATION
The cap ranges from 5–20cm/2–8in across, or even larger. Its light brown colour looks rather like freshly baked bread, hence the name Penny Bun. The colour darkens as the cap opens, and it is at this stage that you should examine specimens for maggot infestation. In wet weather the cap can have a slightly sticky

> **WARNING LOOKALIKES**
> Many boletes look similar and most are edible, if not as good to eat as ceps, though some are rarer and shouldn't be picked for that reason. Bitter boletes are to be avoided, as are of course devil's boletes, which are rare with pale caps and red stems, and found in southern oak woodland.

gently rounded cap, becoming dimpled with age

firm white flesh

light then greeny-yellow pores, which can become spongy

fat stem, white with brown or grey markings

appearance, but in dry weather it has a nice velvety sheen. The stem varies from 4–15cm/ 1½–6in long and 2–5cm/¾–1in wide. It is very bulbous and has a fine network, with markings that are more pronounced towards the cap. The pores are white at first, turning light yellow with age. The flesh is quite white and does not change as the mushroom ages. The spore print is olive-brown.

HABITAT AND SEASON
Found within coniferous, broad-leaved and mixed woodland, as well as along grassy paths close to trees. It can also be found in association with rockrose, dwarf birch and with dwarf willows. The season is summer to late autumn and it is quite common.

STORAGE
Cut into thin slices, this is probably the most important commercially dried mushroom in the world. Take your cue from this – drying is the best method of home storage. Small specimens can be kept in extra-virgin olive oil.

PREPARATION AND COOKING HINTS
Clean the caps well and cut in half to check for maggots before putting them in the basket. Brush the stem, cutting off the bottom or scraping it to remove any earth or fibres at the base. Nutty and substantial, this is one of the most versatile mushrooms. Large specimens can take longer to cook, but also tend to have more flavour (though if too old, they may be better used in soups).

BAY BOLETE
Imleria badia

Previously known as *Boletus badius*. Bay boletes do not become infested with maggots as much as some of the other boletes, but it is still best to pick only clean, young specimens. A common mushroom, the flavour is excellent.

IDENTIFICATION
The cap is 5–15cm/2–6in across and is usually a rich chestnut-brown, although lighter specimens may be found. It has a polished appearance, and feels tacky when wet. The stem is very variable and can be thin to quite swollen, 4–12cm/1½–4½in long and 1.5–3cm/½–1½in wide, smooth and similar in colour to the cap. The pores are light yellow, but stain blue if pressed or cut, which is one of the principal identification features. The white flesh has a faint mushroomy smell, and also stains blue when cut, though this soon fades. The spore print is olive-brown.

HABITAT AND SEASON
In all types of mixed woodland. The season is early summer to late autumn.

Above: The rich bay chestnut colour of the mushroom is the source of its descriptive name.

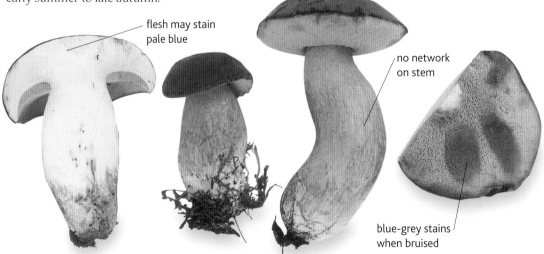

flesh may stain
pale blue

no network
on stem

blue-grey stains
when bruised

STORAGE

Small specimens may be stored in jars of olive oil, or in wine or cider vinegar. Larger specimens are best sliced and dried after the pores have been removed, because these will be quite wet and will not dry satisfactorily. These pores could be used in a mushroom ketchup or sauce.

PREPARATION AND COOKING HINTS

Fresh or dried, the bay boletus is very versatile and can be used in many wild mushroom dishes. They are best picked when dry, as they can become spongy in the rain. Wipe the caps of any wet specimens and let them dry before dealing with them.

Note: Many mushrooms are named bolete but not all are from the Boletus genus. Taxonomic changes are continuing in the *Boletaceae* or Boletus family. Other groups broadly described as boletes in their common names are *Suillus*, *Leccinum* and *Xerocomellus*.

Below left and right: Bay boletes normally have a parallel stem, but occasionally this can appear swollen, which some recognise as a distinct species called *Boletus vaccinus*; this is found under broadleaved trees.

RED CRACKING BOLETE

Xerocomellus chrysenteron (previously known as *Boletus chyrsenteron*). The flavour is not generally considered to be very good, but it is edible, perhaps best used in soups and stews. The cap is a light reddish-brown, but cracks in the surface often reveal a slightly reddish hue below. The red markings on the stem are the real giveaway of this boletus. The pores are yellow and much more open than those of the bay bolete; they slowly stain a light green-blue colour. The flesh is creamy yellow, and the spore print is olive-brown.

BROWN BIRCH BOLETE
Leccinum scabrum

Although brown birch bolete is not as well flavoured as orange birch bolete, it is still quite useful in the kitchen. However, only pick young firm specimens, as older ones tend to absorb moisture and so have a very soft texture.

IDENTIFICATION
The cap is 5–15cm/2–6in across and yellowish brown to dark brown in colour. It is dry, but can be slightly sticky in wet weather. The stem is 7–20cm/2¾–8in long and 2–4cm/¾–1½in wide, white to buff, with grey to blackish and brownish flecked scales. The pores are white, becoming brown with age. The flesh is white, occasionally turning pink on cutting, and the smell is quite pleasant. The spore print is olivaceous brown.

HABITAT AND SEASON
Grows under birch trees. The season is summer to late autumn.

Below: The common name refers to a suite of Leccinum species which are edible but difficult for the beginner to separate. Their scaly (squamulose) stems are a feature.

flesh may redden in some forms

long stem with rough surface

slightly sticky smooth cap

stem can be swollen at base

STORAGE
Drying is the best method of storage. Cut the mushroom into sections and either air-dry or use an electric dryer.

PREPARATION AND COOKING HINTS
As this mushroom has quite a soft watery texture, it is best to use it in conjunction with other mushrooms, in a mixed mushroom dish or in soups.

ORANGE BIRCH BOLETE
Leccinum versipelle

A birch bolete that is particularly flavoursome. It can grow to a fairly large size and, as the name implies, is found close to birch trees.

flesh turns reddish-lilac then black when cut

stem scales darken with handling

leaves of birch, the preferred host tree

IDENTIFICATION
The cap is 8–18cm/3–7in across. It is a lovely orange colour and has a slightly fluffy appearance at first before becoming smooth or scaly, depending on the weather conditions. It is usually dry. The stem can be up to 7–20cm/2¾–8in long and 1.5–5cm/½–2in wide. It is white to greyish in colour and covered with brown to blackish scales. The stems of young specimens bruise blue in patches. Pores are greyish white to almost black when young, then pale brown. The flesh is pale, becoming blackish with age. The smell is quite pleasant. When cut in cross-section this mushroom stains quite black on the inside, but you should not be put off by this as it is good to eat and a useful identification character. The spore print is olivaceous brown.

HABITAT AND SEASON
Grows in association with birch and scrub. The season is midsummer to late autumn.

STORAGE
This is best stored by slicing and drying.

PREPARATION AND COOKING HINTS
It should only be necessary to wipe the cap with a damp cloth and brush any loose dust particles from the stem. This mushroom must be well cooked; it been reported to cause some stomach upsets in some people, so test a little first.

Left: The caps may expand to a much greater size in proportion to the stem than is shown here and the colour can fade to dull yellow buff.

Right: The cap may become quite felt-like and scaly with age.

SLIPPERY JACK
Suillus luteus

Also once known as pine bolete or sticky bun, slippery jack is quite common and a good find, although its open texture makes it prone to maggot infestation. With a delicate taste, it is very versatile in the kitchen.

Only pick mature fresh specimens, and always peel and cook them. There are similar-looking mushrooms you might come across, also edible when peeled, for instance weeping bolete (*Suillus granulatus*) and larch bolete (*S. grevillei*), although most Suillus species associate with pine or larch.

Above: This and other *Suillus* species are only found growing under conifers.

IDENTIFICATION

The cap is 5–12cm/2–4½in across; a nice mid-brown to dark purple-brown colour with a marked sheen. It tends to be very sticky when wet, so is best picked in dry conditions. The stem is 5–10cm/2–4in long and 1.5–3cm/½–1¼in wide, pale yellow with a large, clearly visible ring. The pores are small and pale yellow. The flesh is white to yellow. This mushroom has no particularly distinctive smell. The spore print is olivaceous brown.

Left: The cap colours change from young to old specimens. The purple-brown pales to orange-brown with age.

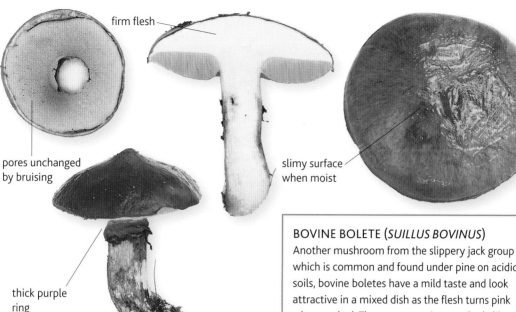

firm flesh

pores unchanged
by bruising

slimy surface
when moist

thick purple
ring

HABITAT AND SEASON
Slippery jack is found exclusively in association
with pine trees. The season is late summer to
late autumn.

STORAGE
Because of its soft texture, this mushroom is
best thinly sliced and dried for use in winter
dishes, or made into a mushroom powder.
Choose young, firm specimens, and remove the
peel and stems.

PREPARATION AND COOKING HINTS
As the cap is slightly sticky in texture and can
disagree when eaten, it should be peeled before
use. Also check the mushroom carefully for
maggot infestation. This mushroom exudes
quite a lot of juice when cooking, so it is a good
idea to sauté it out first on its own. Strain well
and keep the resulting liquid to be used later for
a sauce, perhaps thickened. Slippery jack can be
used in many ways.

BOVINE BOLETE (*SUILLUS BOVINUS*)
Another mushroom from the slippery jack group
which is common and found under pine on acidic
soils, bovine boletes have a mild taste and look
attractive in a mixed dish as the flesh turns pink
when cooked. There are no poisonous lookalikes to
be concerned with, but as with many boletes one
has to be quick to beat the fungus gnats! The
cinnamon, yellow or rusty orange caps are
4–10cm/1½–4in across, viscid when wet but shiny
when dry, with a paler margin which can be
inrolled at first. The stem, 4–6cm/1½–2½in long
and 0.5–1cm/under ½in wide, is smooth and
similar in colour to the cap, cylindrical, sometimes
tapering, often curved at the base and without a
ring. The mycelium attached at the base is pink.
The pores are dirty olive-yellow, quite wide, and
angular or irregular. The flesh is cream to brown,
sometimes pinkish but not bluing. The smell is not
distinctive. The spore print is an olive-brown.

VELVET BOLETE
Suillus variegatus

Also known as variegated bolete, this is another useful bolete to add to your collection, although it is not as good to eat as cep or bay bolete. Only pick young specimens. They are quite light in texture and can become maggot-infested, so check before picking.

Above: The rough, almost dry surface of the cap is seen well here.

IDENTIFICATION
The cap is 6–10cm/2½–4in across and a rusty tawny colour. It is sticky when picked wet. The tawny stem is 6–10cm/2½–4in long and 1.5–2cm/½–¾in wide. The pores are quite clearly a dark yellowish-brown colour. The flesh is yellowish with an orange hue, turning blue in the cap, particularly just above the tubes when cut. The spore print is olivaceous brown.

HABITAT AND SEASON
Found almost exclusively with pine. The season is from late summer to late autumn.

PREPARATION AND COOKING HINTS
A wipe of the cap is usually all that is necessary, but beware when slicing specimens to look out for maggot infestation. A good addition to mixed mushroom dishes.

STORAGE
The velvet bolete is best dried.

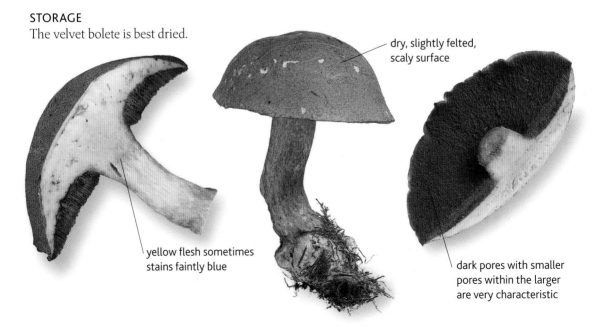

dry, slightly felted, scaly surface

yellow flesh sometimes stains faintly blue

dark pores with smaller pores within the larger are very characteristic

WOOD HEDGEHOG
Hydnum repandum

This little gem is often quite difficult to find on the woodland floor. Perseverance pays as it has great culinary value and is much sought after.

IDENTIFICATION
The caps are usually single and 3–10cm/1¼–4in across, flattening with a slight central depression and rolled rim. They are suede-like to touch. The stem is 2–6cm/¾–2½in long and 1.5–3cm/½–1¼in wide, and quite bulbous. It is quite downy and is white, bruising reddish brown when cut. In place of pores or veins, this mushroom has little spines, hence the name hedgehog. The cap colour can vary from a golden cream to white (rarer) or a pinkish buff. The flesh is white with a very pleasant smell. Its spore print is cream.

HABITAT AND SEASON
Grows under deciduous or coniferous trees, in damp sites such as drainage ditches or in mossy patches. Season is late summer to autumn.

spines on underside of cap

very thick tough stems

thick, peppery-tasting flesh

STORAGE
These are best sliced and dried for winter use, although they can be kept in oil or vinegar.

PREPARATION AND COOKING HINTS
After cleaning, smaller specimens can be cooked whole or else sliced. With larger ones it is probably best to remove the spines, as although quite edible they look like small hairs and could spoil the appearance of the dish. A versatile mushroom, with excellent flavour and texture; younger mushrooms have a peppery quality.

Left: Wood hedgehogs are some of the safest mushrooms to forage for; soft smooth caps and pale spines are hard to mistake for any other fungus.

JELLY EAR
Auricularia auricula-judae

A common fungus with a very long growing season. Other names it can be known by include Tree Ear and Wood Ear. It is related and similar in taste to commercially-bought dried Chinese mushrooms (known as cloud ears).

IDENTIFICATION
The fruitbody is 2–8cm/¾–3in across with a jelly-like texture and an ear-shaped appearance. In dry weather it becomes hard. It is tan-brown with small greyish hairs on the inner surface.

HABITAT AND SEASON
Although most commonly found on elder, jelly ears also grow on sycamore, beech and many other broadleaved trees and shrubs. They have an extremely long growing season and therefore can be collected throughout the year. In summer and through dry periods, these mushrooms shrivel and dry out, but they reconstitute nicely as soon as the wet weather returns.

Above: Starting out as smooth cup shapes, as they age jelly ears become more lobed and misshapen, and darker in colour.

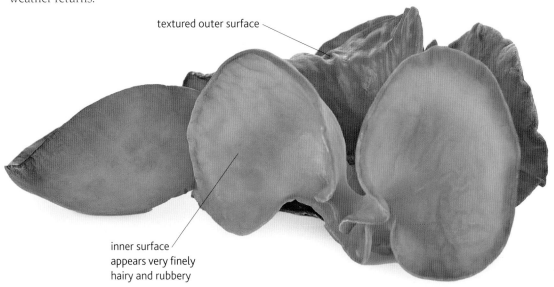

textured outer surface

inner surface appears very finely hairy and rubbery

Right: The colour can vary greatly. These specimens are young and fresh and are quite bright. Jelly ears are delicious if dried, rehydrated in a strong-flavoured liqueur and then dipped in dark chocolate.

STORAGE

Jelly ears are best stored dried. In fact, if they are picked during dry weather when they are hard, they can be stored immediately. Before using, reconstitute them by soaking them for a while in lukewarm water.

PREPARATION AND COOKING HINTS

Wash them thoroughly with several changes of water. As they have quite a gelatinous texture it is important to cook them well, though they do keep their texture. A nice way to serve them is to slice into a sauce made with onions, garlic and basil, thickening it with a little cream. Drying and rehydrating them in a liqueur, then dipping them in dark chocolate, is also an excellent way to serve these mushrooms!

WARNING LOOKALIKE

Some care over identification is necessary, as the jelly ear can look similar to some *Pezizaceae* or cup fungi, some of which are poisonous. However these grow on the floor not trees and don't have the right texture – if in doubt, try stretching it between your fingers; jelly ear should be elastic and rubbery rather than brittle.

GIANT PUFFBALL
Calvatia gigantea

The giant puffball can be truly spectacular. It is also versatile in the kitchen, but only pick specimens that are fresh and young and sound hollow when you tap the top of the mushroom. It is pointless picking this mushroom once the flesh has become discoloured. Check its age by cutting the specimen right through; the knife should not tear the flesh but pass crisply through it.

IDENTIFICATION
The fruitbody can range from 5–80cm/2–32in across, although specimens of 120cm/47in have been recorded. There is no obvious stem. When young it has a clean white appearance, although the outer wall may break away to expose the spore mass and become yellow. Avoid at this stage; we are after young specimens for eating.

HABITAT AND SEASON
It grows in gardens, pastures, woodlands and a wide variety of other situations, such as along stream banks. The season is any time from early summer to late autumn unless the weather is very dry, when it will not grow. There will usually be several in the same area and they grow in the same place year after year, sometimes in large rings.

STORAGE
There is no satisfactory way of storing giant puffballs, so it is best to make up the dishes and freeze them.

PREPARATION AND COOKING HINTS
Very little needs to be done to this mushroom. Wipe the specimens carefully with a damp cloth and, if you are not going to use them immediately, wrap in cling film and keep in the refrigerator for up to 3 days. The giant puffball goes extremely well in all wild mushroom dishes, perhaps better fried than simmered in soups and stews. It makes a good breakfast sliced and fried, or dipped in beaten egg and breadcrumbs and lightly fried.

the outer skin can be almost suede-like to touch

Below: Hedges and ditch banks are favourite habitats of giant puffball.

solid white flesh when young

OTHER PUFFBALLS

You are more likely to spot the smaller common puffball than the giant, and there are a number of mushrooms given variants of the same common name, although they are scientifically allocated to specific genera or groups. The 'puff' of their names refers less to their puffy rounded appearance as to the way many release their spores, puffing them out through a little hole, a process which can be observed when a raindrop lands on a mature puffball and triggers their release.

Lycoperdon excipuliforme (*Handkea excipuliformis*) is commonly known as the pestle or long-stemmed puffball, and frequently grows in large clusters in woodlands. It is edible but best picked young with all-white flesh; the skin can be tough so is usually peeled. The common puffball (*Lycoperdon perlatum*), also found in woodlands, has a short, squat stem and distinctive little spines, which break off but leave markings on the ovoid cap. The meadow puffball (*Lycoperdon pratense*) is smooth and white so can look similar to the giant, though it has a stem and is smaller, reaching about 4cm/1½in. There is also the stump puffball (*Apioperdon pyriforme*), which grows in clusters on tree stumps.

> ### WARNING LOOKALIKE
> Because they are also round balls, there can be mistaken identification with poisonous earthballs, *Scleroderma*. The inside colour is the main teller, as the puffball is pure white whereas earthballs have a black marbled interior.

Below: Another large edible puffball, the pestle, *Lycoperdon excipuliforme*.

Below left: *Lycoperdon pratense*, meadow puffball.

Below right: *Lycoperdon perlatum*, common puffball.

CHANTERELLE
Cantharellus cibarius

The excitement of finding this fungus (known as the girolle in some countries) is, for many, the highlight of the mushroom season – not only does it look beautiful, it tastes wonderful. Most collectors are secretive about their chanterelle patches because these mushrooms grow year after year, often in abundant quantities. It is important to be sure you have found the true chanterelle and not simply the false chanterelle.

IDENTIFICATION
The cap is 2–12cm/¾–4½in across. Flat at first with a incurved irregular margin, it later becomes quite fluted or funnel-like, with a central depression and wavey, lobed margin. The colour can range from very pale to deep yellow, fading a little with age. The stem is 3–8cm/1¼–3in long and 0.5–1.5cm/¼–½in wide, very solid and tapered towards the base. The yellow gill-like folds or veins are blunt, narrow, irregular and run down the stem. The yellowish flesh can have a faint fragrance of apricots – and tastes peppery if chewed raw. The spore print is a pale cream.

Above: The 'folds' run down the stem and are the same colour as the cap.

Below: The gill-like folds are very shallow, blunt and often forked, more like deep wrinkles than true gills.

WARNING LOOKALIKES
The most likely pretender is clear from its name, the false chanterelle *Hygrophoropsis aurantiaca* (pictured below), unfortunately common. Orange rather than yellow, it has an inrolled edge to the cap, and true gills. The jack o'lantern (*Omphalotus illudens*) grows in clumps on tree stumps and can look a little similar, but is rarely seen in the UK.

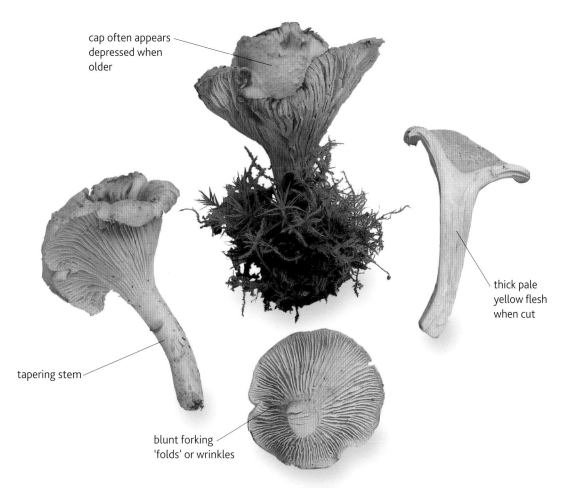

cap often appears depressed when older

thick pale yellow flesh when cut

tapering stem

blunt forking 'folds' or wrinkles

HABITAT AND SEASON

Found in all kinds of woodland that have open mossy clearings, particularly wet woodland. Often found growing in groups, chanterelles like beech, oak, birch and pine trees. Slow growing, their season is early summer to late autumn.

STORAGE

The chanterelle has a good shelf life: specimens can be kept fresh for some time either in a refrigerator or in a cool, airy place. All forms of storage can be recommended, including drying. It is an interesting one to store in spiced liquor because of its fragrant flavour, but is equally good stored in extra-virgin olive oil or vinegar.

PREPARATION AND COOKING HINTS

It is important to clean chanterelles well when you pick them. Brush the caps, and wipe them with a damp cloth if necessary. Cut the stem to avoid any dirt getting into your basket. The beautifully shaped and intensely coloured chanterelle has an appealing scent of apricot with a hint of citrus. They taste exquisite and are extremely versatile, whether on their own, in mixed mushroom dishes or with meat or fish dishes. They also give an elegant colour to sauces and the overall appearance of a dish. Try mixing different types of *Cantharellus* for a brilliant combination of colours, flavours and textures.

HORN OF PLENTY
Craterellus cornucopioides

Also known as black trumpets, trompette de morts (somewhat off-puttingly) and black chanterelle, horn of plenty is another wonderful woodland mushroom of the Chanterelle family. Like chanterelle and trumpet chanterelle, horn of plenty appears in large groups in the same place year after year. They are quite often covered by dead leaves and therefore hard to spot because of their colour. Although the initial appearance is not inviting, the taste is excellent.

IDENTIFICATION
The cap is 2–8cm/¾–3in across, and 8–10cm/3–4in (or more) tall; it is shaped like a tube or a trumpet and has an open flared mouth and is hollow. It becomes irregular with age and is thin and tough. In colour it ranges from mid-brown to black, though it fades with age. The veins are barely perceptible. The flesh is grey to black. The spore print is pale cream.

HABITAT AND SEASON
Grows in old deciduous woods from late summer to late autumn, particularly around beech and oak trees. If you spot one, there are likely more around. Although this species is quite common in old woodland, it can be mistaken for the rare *Cantharellus cinereus* (ashen chanterelle) which looks similar but has more pronounced wrinkled veins.

trumpet-like depression

smooth to slightly wrinkled surface

STORAGE
All forms of storage are appropriate for horn of plenty, but it is probably best dried, which intensifies its subtle flavour.

PREPARATION AND COOKING HINTS
Remember that these mushrooms are hollow. You will always need to brush them and, with larger specimens, it is best to slice them in half and remove any debris that has gone down the funnel-cap. Horn of plenty has a sweet earthy richness that goes a long way to flavour soups and stews; its black colour does not bleed even after long cooking. It is very versatile, but goes particularly well with white fish, making a striking colour contrast.

completely hollow

Below: Like trumpet or winter chanterelle, this species is typically found on damp mossy banks alongside streams and in deep leaf mould.

WARNING LOOKALIKES
A common lookalike is *Russula nigricans*, blackening brittlegill. Old fruitbodies are also often mistaken for horn of plenty, but a closer look reveals gills.

TRUMPET CHANTERELLE
Craterellus tubaeformis

Previously known as *Cantharellus tubaeformis* and also *Cantharellus infundibuliformis,* trumpet or winter chanterelle usually appears much later than ordinary chanterelle. It has other common names too, winter chanterelle, and funnel chanterelle. It is quite an achievement to find these tiny little gems hidden under falling autumn leaves of the same yellowy brown colour. But once you get your eye in, you will spot groups of them growing where before you had hardly seen anything. They tend to grow in the same place each year, so make a good note where you find them. A good tip is to follow woodland streams and their mossy banks.

greyish-lilac
forked veins or
wrinkles

tough long,
thin stems

Above: When growing in fallen leaves, trumpet chanterelles are very difficult to spot.

WARNING LOOKALIKES
Avoid confusing *Craterellus tubaeformis* with *Craterellus lutescens*, a rare fungus often found in Scottish pine forests that should not be picked.

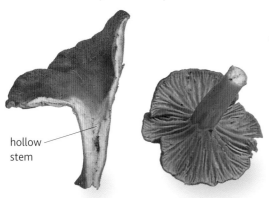

hollow stem

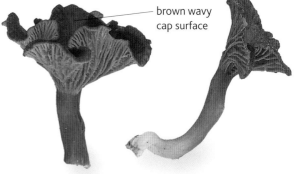

brown wavy cap surface

IDENTIFICATION
The cap is 2–6cm/¾–2½in across, convex at first, soon becoming funnel-shaped with an irregular wavy margin. It is yellowish to dark brown on top. The stem is 5–8cm/2–3in long and 0.5–0.8cm/¼–½in wide, yellow to grey, and hollow. The vein-like gills are narrow, branching and irregular, yellowish becoming greyish-lilac with age. The flesh is yellowish and smells faintly sweet. The spore print is yellowish cream.

HABITAT AND SEASON
Grows in large numbers in both deciduous and coniferous woods. The season is from late summer to late autumn.

STORAGE
Trumpet chanterelles dry extremely well, but can also be stored in olive oil or wine vinegar.

PREPARATION AND COOKING HINTS
As these usually grow through leaf mould they are quite clean, so all they are likely to need is a dusting with your brush. If you cut the stalks rather than pulling them up, you will avoid earth and other debris. This mushroom has a rich mossy scent that combines well with other mushrooms. After trimming at the base, it is best used whole. It is very versatile in cooking, with a nice, sweet flavour that goes especially well with fish.

DRYAD'S SADDLE
Cerioporus squamosus

Intriguing in appearance, this mushroom has large brown scales rather like pheasant feathers, and grows out of the bark of trees. A common bracket fungus, it appears in late spring and into summer but only the young soft mushrooms are edible – if you are struggling to cut it with a knife, it will be tough to chew when cooked!

IDENTIFICATION:
The cap is a cream to ochre colour and has a fan-shaped pattern or dark concentric scales,

Below: Often found on old logs of broadleaved trees. Note the strong smell of watermelon from the pores.

and can grow as large as 60cm/24in across and 5cm/2in thick. Often several brackets are branched from the same base.

Initially circular, the mushroom quickly develops a lateral stem and becomes quite corky in appearance. The stem appears white to creamy because it is mostly covered by the pores, but is black towards the base.

The underside of the cap is covered in large angular pores which are decurrent and stretch right down the stem.

Dryad's sadddle has white to cream flesh which smells of watermelon. The spore print is white.

Above: This is the ideal stage at which to collect; as the brackets get larger they quickly get quite 'woody' but still make excellent mushroom powder for stock.

Below: They are are important habitats for many invertebrates, so never collect all the brackets you find.

HABITAT AND SEASON
Parasitic on wounds of broadleaved trees, most commonly sycamore, beech, ash and elm.

STORAGE
It is recommended that you cook this mushroom straight away as it loses its aroma and taste within a day of picking. This mushroom dries well and can be powdered to make a mushroom stock.

PREPARATION AND COOKING HINTS
Use young fresh specimens which can easily be sliced, as this mushroom quickly gets quite tough and unpalatable. To prepare, simply wipe clean, cut off any very hard stems or scales, and slice. Cook this mushroom thoroughly, as undercooking can cause some stomach upsets.

BEEFSTEAK FUNGUS
Fistulina hepatica

This unusual and charismatic bracket is most often found on old oak or sweet chestnut trees, even dead fallen ones. It can be found anywhere on the trunk of the tree, but it's worth keeping a roll of tape in your pocket for brackets like beefsteak and chicken of the woods. You can use the tape to attach the knife to a stick to extend your reach. Looking and bleeding like a steak, there's no other fungus like it.

IDENTIFICATION
The bracket can vary from 8–30cm/3–12in across and is quite thick. It is usually in a single piece, although several may grow one above the other. Cut through, beefsteak fungus really does look rather like a piece of meat. The colour of the bracket is an orange-red darkening with age; the pores underneath are much lighter. The flesh is thick, fibrous, succulent and often a mottled dark red; it has quite a pleasant smell. The spore print is a pinkish cream.

Above The upper surface can be very moist and spongy when fresh.

Left: Another good clue to identifying this species is that the individual tubes separate from each other very easily, unlike all other bracket fungi.

pores pull apart
very easily

cut flesh 'bleeds'
red juice

HABITAT AND SEASON

Grows on oak or chestnut trees, usually, but not always, on the lower part of the trunk. Season is late summer to autumn, although it may appear earlier. Although this fungus causes rot inside a tree it does not kill it, but it makes the wood of infected trees much darker. Oak darkened in this way is in demand in the furniture and wood-working industry.

STORAGE

This bracket is excellent if dried as jerky. Otherwise, it is best used fresh as one would cook meat.

PREPARATION AND COOKING HINTS

Cut off any parts of the tree still attached to the fungus. Separate the various layers and wipe them with a damp cloth. It is best brushed with chipotle or a strong sweet vinegar (elderberry is good) and dried in a dehydrator for jerky, but it can also be sliced and cooked like meat. It works

well on a BBQ but although it has a slightly bitter taste, this can be balanced by brining or with a sweet marinade. It is excellent added to soups and stews for extra flavour and colour. For a mushroom 'port', chop and steep in vodka for a couple of weeks, then strain off and blend with a berry liqueur and sugar.

Right: Beefsteak fungus are more usually found at the tree base but they can grow high up on the trunks.

HEN OF THE WOODS
Grifola frondosa

Previously known as *Polyporus frondosus*, this is an unusual fungus which, like cauliflower fungus, grows at the base of tree trunks and can be extremely large. Its many caps are joined together and a large specimen can provide a feast for many people. It is good to eat and quite rare, so note where you find it as it will certainly grow there again. It is not related to chicken of the woods (see page 108).

IDENTIFICATION
The fruitbody is 20–50cm/8–20in across, and consists of a central section with many branch stems ending in individual caps. Each cap is 3–8cm/1–3in across and has quite a wrinkled edge. The whole fruitbody is greyish in colour turning brown with age. The stems are white to grey-brown. Hen of the woods has pores rather than gills, spaced roughly 2–4mm/under ¼in,

Above and right: Look for small overlapping caps and flesh that does not turn brown when bruised.

and which run down the stem. The tube length is up to 5mm/¼in long. The flesh, which is white, has a slightly musty smell.

HABITAT AND SEASON
Hen of the woods grows at the base of the trunks of oaks or other deciduous trees. Occasionally it grows on tree stumps. The season is autumn to early winter.

STORAGE
The best method of storage is drying. It can be smoked and powdered to use as a versatile flavouring. Otherwise prepare and then freeze your cooked dishes.

PREPARATION AND COOKING HINTS
It is important to clean this thoroughly as it has many nooks and crevices which harbour dirt. Due to its very tough texture it can be rinsed in cold water prior to cooking. It tastes good and goes well in a wide variety of dishes, but,

Above: The brackets consist of a large number of frondose-stemmed lobes.

because of its tough texture, make sure it is well cooked. These often large brackets can easily feed a group, but they tend to have good and bad years, making them quite unpredictable. Hen of the woods lend themselves well to smoking, and make a useful condiment if dried and powdered.

GIANT POLYPORE

Lookalike giant polypore *Meripilus giganteus* is the fungus most often confused with hen of the woods. Giant polypore often grows larger, with broader lobes that are yellow to red/brown, bruising brown/black on handling. It is often found at the base of beech trees. When very young, it is also considered edible.

CHICKEN OF THE WOODS
Laetiporus sulphureus

One of the more spectacular of all bracket fungi, this can grow in very large quantities and comes quite early in the mushroom season. Its versatility makes it important from a culinary point of view, but only pick young specimens. It is not related to hen of the woods (see page 106).

IDENTIFICATION
The bracket can be 15–50cm/6–20in across. Often the shape of a fan, it has a semi-circular growing habit and rounded edges. The colour is spectacular: lemon to orange- yellow, although it tends to darken with age. The brackets have an almost velvet-like appearance. Young specimens exude a yellow, pungent juice.

HABITAT AND SEASON
Grows on deciduous trees, particularly oak and sweet chestnut. It may also be found on yew and various conifers as well as eucalyptus. Some believe that this mushroom is poisonous when found on yew and eucalyptus, however, there is no evidence that the fungus picks up toxins from these trees; any poisoning is probably due to people eating the woodier old growth nearest the tree; only fresh growth from the margin should be collected and all traces of tree cut off. The season is late spring to early autumn, but if the winter has been mild it can appear earlier.

Below: When young, it can look quite strange and lumpy.

older specimens tend to become quite woody with a uniform dull yellow pallor

velvety surface

STORAGE

Drying toughens this mushroom, so it is best used fresh and the finished dish frozen.

PREPARATION AND COOKING HINTS

Avoid the toughest specimens and only use young ones. Cleaning can be difficult but it is best to separate the individual layers, brushing lightly, bearing in mind that the dense texture makes it possible to wash it to remove any infestation or dirt. If you notice a slight bitter taste blanch it for 2–3 minutes in boiling, salted water prior to cooking. The texture and flavour is of chicken, as the name suggests, and it is much prized by chefs. It is wonderful for vegetarian meals. It has been known to disagree with some people, so ensure it is well cooked, and test a small amount first.

WARNING LOOKALIKE

Phaeolus schweinitzii (dyer's mazegill) is another large yellow bracket fungi, usually browner and hairier, found at the base or on roots of conifers. It isn't poisonous but inedible, to be avoided.

Right: The bracket lasts quite a while in the field and as it ages becomes softer, spongier and paler in colour. Pick the young, brightly coloured fruitbodies.

Below: Only collect young specimens with orange and sulphur tones, and collect the leading part of the bracket away from the tree.

CAULIFLOWER FUNGUS
Sparassis crispa

Cauliflower fungus is quite unlike any other fungus you will find in the woods. When you find one you will understand why it got its name. (It is also known colloquially as the brain fungus, sea sponge, the ruffle, and wood cauliflower.) It is quite unusual, but can grow in the same place year after year, so make a note of where you find it. One large specimen can last for several days if stored carefully in a cool place with its base in water. You could also cut off just the part you intend to use, if it is very large, and leave the rest to grow.

IDENTIFICATION
Cauliflower fungus has no cap in the ordinary sense of the word. Instead the fruitbody is built up of many layers resembling a cauliflower or a brain. A short stem attaches it to the tree on which it grows. The fruitbody ranges from 20–50cm/8–20in in diameter. It ages from a pale yellow-white to brown. It has a sweet smell and a wonderful nutty flavour.

HABITAT AND SEASON
This grows on the base of living and dead conifers, most frequently pine, and is even found on cut stumps. Cauliflower fungus grows from late summer to late autumn but is susceptible to frosts and so will be killed by the first hard frosts of winter.

Sparassis crispa is a widespread species; another species with a more southern distribution is called *S. spathulata* and is slightly pinkish and lacks a stem. It grows on old oak stumps. Please do not pick this one in Britain, as it is very rare.

STORAGE
This dries extremely well. Air-drying is probably best: hang your specimens up on strings in a light, airy place for several days. Very large specimens can be cut into sections so they will dry more quickly. As the fungi dry the insects and other life in them will fall out, so do not attempt to dry them in your kitchen; an airy

colour varies from buff to creamy white

edges of lobes turn brown with age

Above: The fruit bodies are almost always at the base of a tree or stump.

Above: Note the flattened crispy lobes. If they are pointed and branched you have probably mistakenly picked one of the similar-looking *Ramaria* species, which can be toxic.

shed or outside storeroom would be best. Any hint of dampness will, of course, spoil the drying. It is very important to dry thoroughly.

WARNING LOOKALIKE
The rare coral fungi in the *Ramaria* group have a superficial resemblance to cauliflower fungus but are toxic to eat. Some *Ramaria* species are uncommon and have thinner longer strands, more akin to coral, as you'd expect.

PREPARATION AND COOKING HINTS
Pick only creamy white specimens, as this is when the fungus will be at its very best. Cleaning needs care as there are so many nooks and crannies in the cauliflower fungus and, as it grows so close to the ground pine needles can be a problem. If possible, avoid cleaning in water. It is better to brush away any dust particles, then cut into thin slices and clean each slice before cooking. If you do use water, remember to dry the fungus well on paper towels before cooking.

Perhaps known for its lovely crisp texture more than its flavour, one of the nicest ways to deal with this fungus is to cut it in thin slices, dip them in a batter made with beer rather than milk, and deep-fry to make a wonderfully crisp nutty snack, or accompaniment to a favourite dish. But it is also good sliced fresh and added to stews and casseroles.

BLACK MOREL
Morchella elata/conica

Morels are among the most exciting springtime fungi – see also overleaf for the common morel. Morels can be quite hard to spot because they blend into their background so well. They usually grow singly but can sometimes be found in clusters. Although they are excellent mushrooms from the culinary point of view, morels must be cooked before eating – never, ever eat them raw.

IDENTIFICATION
Morchella elata/conica is now known to be a complex group of several species and includes

Below: Black morels may be found in coniferous woodlands as well as along paths and in gardens.

its American cousin *M. importuna,* which is often found in woodchip and bark mulches in towns and gardens. All the species appear almost identical, despite the variation in their DNA. They are similar to *M. esculenta* or common morel but, as the name suggests, much darker, often almost black with the ridges and pits aligned in vertical rows. The cap is often tall and pointed. The mushroom stands 5–15cm/2–6in high and is always hollow; the stem is white and almost smooth.

HABITAT AND SEASON
Grows in coniferous woodland, mostly on calcareous soils, gardens, wood chippings, waste ground, along roadsides and disused railway

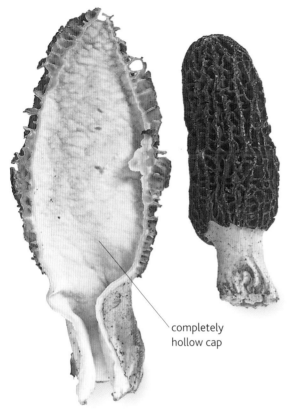

completely
hollow cap

Above: The morels love camouflaging themselves on forest floor and bark chippings and can be hard to see. The dark caps of this group have neat ladder-like patterning; the lighter *M. esculenta* has more irregular honeycombed pits and ridges.

WARNING LOOKALIKE
The false morel, or *Gyromitra esculenta*, isn't very common but is highly poisonous. It has a superficial similarity to a dark morel, but the cap shape is irregular and more contorted..

lines. In fact, they are found more often nowadays in urban wasteland areas and in the chipping mulches of park beds and borders. The season is throughout the spring.

STORAGE
Like *Morchella esculenta*, black morel is best dried for storing.

PREPARATION AND COOKING HINTS
Clean your black morels thoroughly before cooking, slicing the fruitbody in half to make sure it is free of insects, such as woodlice. Cook and serve as you would *Morchella esculenta* (though it is not quite as flavourful), and, like that morel, it must be properly cooked. Both fresh and dried are prized for their tobacco-rich scent of sulphur and oak.

MOREL
Morchella esculenta

Another member of the highly edible morel family. This one, like the slightly more common black morel *Morchella elata/conica* group (see previous page), is one of the earlier mushrooms to appear in spring, so keep an eye open for it.

IDENTIFICATION
M. esculenta is now understood to represent a group of species which are hard to separate, and thought to be saprosymbiotic (saprotrophs that can sometimes establish biotrophic symbiosis with plants). The fruitbody is 5–25cm/2–10in high. Although very convoluted, with a honeycomb effect, the overall shape of the cap can be conical to almost round. It is palish brown or grey and darkens to orange-yellow with age. The length and thickness of the stem can also be variable, white to cream, and hollow inside. This morel has a pleasant spicy smell.

HABITAT AND SEASON
Found among shrubs or in open woodland, on rich, often calcareous ground with elm, poplar and ash. The season is throughout the spring. The large but slightly darker *Morchella vulgaris* is very similar but prefers broadleaved forests, parks, gardens and sand dunes.

STORAGE
Best dried for storage. Clean thoroughly.

young caps are darker

pits and ridges are very irregular, never in vertical lines as in the black morel

completely hollow cap and stem

older caps are quite yellow

stem base often very swollen

cap joins stem without overhang

Above: The honeycomb pattern of the cap in this group, which includes *Morchella vulgaris*, can be very variable, appearing from grey to orange.

Right: When young, the fruitbody is often dull buff or brown in colour with blunt ridges.

Far right: When mature, the colour changes to ochre or orange-yellow and the ridges become sharper.

PREPARATION AND COOKING HINTS

Because of all the nooks and crannies, morels are often infested with insects. The easiest way to clean is to slice in half to make sure there is nothing hiding inside, rinse in clear water and dry. One of the nicest ways to use fresh morels is to stuff the large fruitbody. They also go well with meat dishes and provide a very rich sauce. Dried, the intensity of their flavour increases. It must always be properly cooked before eating.

WARNING LOOKALIKE

As shown on page 113, there is a similar mushroom, aptly called false morel, which is not so common but deadly to eat. There are a number of 'false morels' that are considered inedible (unless treated in a very particular way, so not advised for the casual forager-cook), but *Gyromitra esculenta* is especially dangerous.

ORANGE PEEL FUNGUS
Aleuria aurantia

Above: The orange inner surface (the hymenium) contains the spore-producing cells which are called asci.

Left: Often growing in large clusters, orange peel fungus prefers disturbed soils along paths and tracks.

This wonderfully bright fungus has a nice taste and texture. It is a useful addition to many wild mushroom dishes, imparting flavour and colour.

IDENTIFICATION
The fruit body is small, just under 0.5–5cm/¼–2in across; it is cup-shaped and becomes quite wavy at the edges. The inner surface is bright orange in colour. The underside is much lighter and almost velvety to the touch. As is typical within the *ascomycete* or spore-shooting group, spores are formed within the cup and will be fired up into the moving air. The orientation of the cap is a good clue.

HABITAT AND SEASON
Orange peel fungus grows in fairly large clumps on almost bare earth in light grassland, along roads and in lawns. It is quite common and the season is from autumn through to early winter.

STORAGE
Drying is the best method of storage.

PREPARATION AND COOKING HINTS
Apart from cleaning it carefully, orange peel fungus needs very little done to it. It is fairly tough, so can be lightly rinsed in water, then sliced thinly and added to your dishes.

SUMMER TRUFFLE
Tuber aestivum

A round, hard lumpy stone-like fungus that cuts open to reveal an intricate marbled maze. Although summer truffles grow far more extensively than people realise, finding them is difficult for they grow beneath the soil surface.

Tuber aestivum could be mistaken for *T. brumale*, winter truffle, or *T. macrosporum*, large spore truffle. Both are considered edible and good. There are several common false truffles also found in Britain (see box). One should be careful not to confuse any type of truffle with the poisonous earthball group, *Scleroderma* (see note on page 95).

IDENTIFICATION
The fruitbody is 2.5–9cm/1–3½in across. It is irregular, though roughly globe-shaped, and covered in a host of tiny black pyramid-shaped warts. It is blackish-brown in colour. When cut through, it reveals a wonderfully marbled, whitish interior which becomes yellowish to olive-brown. The smell is very distinctive and sweet, and the taste is nutty.

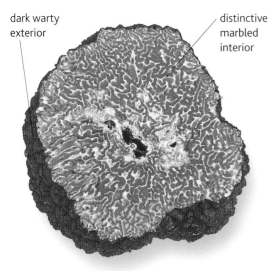

dark warty exterior

distinctive marbled interior

LOOKALIKES
Elaphomyces spp., sometimes referred to as false truffles or deer truffles, are inedible and tough, although deer and squirrels might disagree! There is currently no evidence that they are poisonous. They vary from yellow to brown/black, and can be smooth or ornamented with warts. Their smell is usually slight and unremarkable. The most common, *E. granulatus* and *E. muricatus*, are brown/black with rounded warts, ranging from 1–4cm/½–1½in in diameter.

HABITAT AND SEASON
This truffle favours calcareous soils and can be found in the ground near beech trees, and also, though less often, in association with sweet chestnuts and evergreen oaks. The season is late summer to autumn.

STORAGE
One of the best ways of storing truffles is preserving them in olive oil. First of all clean the truffle and shave off the skin which can be used in future recipes. Blanch the truffles very quickly before placing in oil in an airtight container.

PREPARATION AND COOKING HINTS
As truffles have a very strong flavour they are best used in small amounts and even a tiny quantity can transform a dish. They are delicious served with egg and pasta dishes.

POISONOUS MUSHROOMS

Every year, despite repeated warnings, people die of mushroom poisoning. Such deaths emphasise the importance of identifying your mushrooms correctly. People often make the literally fatal mistake of assuming that if animals can eat a mushroom, then so can humans. Unfortunately, this is untrue. Different organisms have different digestive systems and just because a slug has taken chunks out of a deathcap or another poisonous mushroom, it does not mean that either you or your dog can.

There are many old tales and folklore about how to identify edible and poisonous mushrooms. They are false. Ignore them all and take great care over identification so that you can be sure of living to enjoy your mushroom trophies. The only way to determine whether as mushroom is edible is to know which mushroom it is and then to consult a reference book to find out whether it is considered edible.

Between the popular edible mushrooms and the poisonous, there is an enormous range of other mushrooms regarded as inedible, not worthwhile, or too rare to pick. These are not all included in this book. Should you wish to learn more about them, consult one of the resources listed at the end.

Left: A typical group of fly agarics, *Amanita muscaria*.

MUSHROOMS TO AVOID

If one is prepared to invest the right amount of care in collecting and identifying mushrooms, a poisoning incident should never occur. So why or how do people get poisoned? The first and most obvious cause is a lack of determined scrutiny. In a letter from the victim of a tragic and heart-wrenching near-fatal poisoning, the correspondent claimed to have been collecting porcini (ceps, or penny buns). These mushrooms have spongy pores below their caps, but the species which nearly claimed his life and the lives of other members of his family, was a gilled fungus, a webcap. The victim later referred to a suspension of responsibility between himself and another family member in the identification of the mushroom. This incident demonstrates the importance of being honest with yourself and others regarding your expertise and the amount of care invested in your identification.

Another way to fall foul of a poisonous mushroom is to mistake it for something you feel confident that you know. This can occur when you forage in localities or countries where you are unfamiliar with the local mushrooms. Deathcaps have been fatally mistaken in the UK for paddy straw mushrooms, *Volvariella volvacea,* a mushroom commonly collected, eaten, and commercially cultivated in Asia. Both species grow from a volva and have free gills. The latter has pink spores, unlike the white-spored *Amanita*, and lacks a ring on its stem which is characteristic of deathcaps. However, careless handling can destroy evidence of rings, and rashness can give rise to bad practice with spore prints either not collected or ignored. It is important to always use a local guidebook and ideally forage with a local expert if you are unfamiliar with a region.

Poisonous mushrooms can get picked accidentally. In amongst a carpet of autumn chanterelle, a small poisonous webcap can be disguised and if one is picking enthusiastically or is distracted, the imposter can be collected by mistake. This is exactly what was recently discovered within a punnet of wild mushrooms provided to a well-known supermarket by a professional supplier. It is important to take your time collecting mushrooms and make sure that everything you collect is what you intended to.

As previously discussed, some people do have unique adverse reactions to fungi which are otherwise considered edible. Mushrooms which are past their best can also cause upset stomachs, as can undercooked meals. Fungi sprayed with chemicals could also make you very unwell.

Of course, regardless of how it is that one has become poisoned, it is important to seek medical advice as quickly as is feasible. If possible, take a sample of the type of mushroom that you have eaten to the hospital. Prompt and fastidious identification of the poisoning syndrome can be lifesaving if the correct treatment can be administered rapidly.

Left: The deathcap, *Amanita phalloides*. The slight radial streaking on the cap can be seen well here.

TYPES OF MUSHROOM POISONING

Various types of mushroom poisoning can present quite distinctive symptoms and take different times from consumption to onset of symptoms, all of which can help to identify the poisoning syndrome.

POISONING WITH A DELAYED ONSET OF SYMPTOMS

The most serious poisoning syndromes are caused by cytolytic (cell-damaging) toxins. These typically have a delayed onset of symptoms, reflecting the period it takes our bodies to metabolise the unwelcome compounds, which involve cyclopeptides (amotoxins), orellanine or gyromitrin. These toxins characteristically attack the liver or kidneys, although gyromitrin is also an intoxicant of the central nervous system.

The amatoxins are most often associated with *Amanita virosa* and *A. phalloides* but amatoxins are also found in dapperlings, *Lepiota* spp.; funeral bells and related species, *Galerina* spp.; and conecaps, *Conocybe* spp. Typically, symptoms such as vomiting, abdominal cramps and diarrhoea generally appear within 8–12 hours of ingestion but can be as early as 6 hours in extreme cases or not appear for up to 36 hours in mild cases. These symptoms can subside quite quickly after 24 hours and are often followed by a period of remission. Abdominal symptoms recur by 72 hours after the original ingestion and are accompanied by convulsions, coma, and evidence of organ damage, particularly the liver. In severe poisoning cases, death from liver and kidney failure occurs 7–10 days after the initial symptoms appear.

Orellanine poisoning is caused by species of the webcap group, *Cortinarius orellanus* and *C. rubellus*. Onset of gastroenteritis (nausea, vomiting, and loss of appetite) is at least 12 hours after ingestion, often much longer (2–17 days), followed by increased urination, acute thirst, headache, coldness, shivering, lethargy, muscle and joint pain, and evidence of progressive kidney failure such as gradual decrease in urine output, sometimes finally ceasing altogether. In mild to moderate cases damage to kidneys may be reversible with only temporary, mild renal failure. Deaths are rare due to the general availability of kidney dialysis, but kidney transplantation and chronic dialysis may be required. Other webcap species are also known to cause kidney failure, but the toxins are not yet understood.

Cases of Gyromitrin Syndrome (Monomethyl hydrazine) typically occur in the spring, reflecting the fruiting season of species from the *Gyromitra* and *Morchella* groups. In these cases there is frequently quite a sudden onset of gastroenteritis (vomiting, with or without diarrhoea), usually 6–8 hours after eating, but as is often the case in extreme poisonings, this may occur earlier. These symptoms are sometimes accompanied by fever, severe headache, feeling of fullness and bloating, and abdominal pain with muscle cramps. Most cases do not progress past this stage and recovery usually occurs within a few days, but some symptoms may continue for up to a week.

In the more serious cases of poisoning, a second phase can develop after 36–48 hours, occasionally preceded by a brief period of relative well-being. This second phase is often characterised by jaundice, sometimes with evidence of liver damage, fever, and occasionally kidney failure. In the most extreme cases a terminal phase can progress quite rapidly to coma, circulatory collapse, and respiratory arrest.

Other cases of poisoning with delayed onset of symptoms include Ergotism Syndrome – caused by consumption of ergot-infected rye grain. Typically, there is an incubation period in excess of 8 hours. Toxins affect the central nervous system, causing convulsions and hallucinations. Another form of ergotism known as St Antony's Fire develops when small amounts, usually as flour, are consumed over a long period, causing burning and tingling sensations particularly in fingers and toes. This is caused by the constriction of blood vessels, which can lead to gangrene.

Another example is haemolytic anaemia which is caused by under-cooked blushers, *Amanita rubescens*. Usually, it is over 4 hours before symptoms appear. Poisoning by haemolytic compounds is characterised by the destruction of red blood cells faster than they can be produced by the body, which can lead to anaemia. Symptoms include pallor, and in exceptional cases, kidney blockage. Haemolysins are heat-labile and the fungi containing these agents are only dangerous when eaten raw or undercooked.

As already mentioned, it is important to cook *all* mushrooms. Many heat-labile toxins are found in mushrooms which are considered good to eat. These species include the morels, honey fungus, blewits, chicken of the woods, milkcaps and brittlegills.

POISONING WITH A RAPID ONSET OF SYMPTOMS

However, several types of poisonings have a rapid onset of symptoms. The fastest and most dramatic is caused by Coprine Syndrome, a type of poisoning experienced by people eating common inkcaps, although other inkcaps are also known to contain coprines. Symptoms develop within 5 to 10 minutes after ingestion when consumed with or after previous consumption of alcohol. These can include a metallic taste, sensation of warmth, sweating, blushing, and swelling of the face and neck, anxiety, vertigo, confusion, rapid heart rate,

Above: *Amanita phalloides*.

Above: *Amanita virosa*.

Above: *Lepiota subincarnata*.

Above: *Galerina marginata*.

Above: *Gyromitra esculenta*.

Above: *Cortinarius rubellus*.

palpitations and chest pains, nausea, vomiting, diarrhoea, and sometimes collapse. Symptoms normally resolve in 2–3 hours depending on the quantity of alcohol/mushrooms consumed but can last up to 8 hours and will recur if alcohol is consumed again within 72 hours. The severity in each succeeding episode is usually diminishing. Other fungi known to cause problems when consumed with alcohol are *Suillellus luridus* lurid bolete, *Ampulloclitocybe clavipes* club foot, *Armillaria* spp. honey fungus, and *Pholiota squarosa* shaggy scalycap.

A more severe type of rapid onset poisoning is caused by muscarine, a compound found in fly agaric mushrooms, *Amanita muscaria*. Fly agarics only contain a small amount of the toxin, but funnel caps, *Clitocybe* spp. and allies and fibrecaps, *Inocybe* spp. can contain significant quantities. Onset of symptoms is rapid and often within 15–30 minutes. Certainly within 1 hour almost all cases will manifest symptoms. These vary depending on the quantity consumed, but can include sweating, flushing of the skin, increase salivation, excessive tear production, colicky abdominal pain, nausea, vomiting, diarrhoea, and blurred vision. A significant decrease in blood pressure is usually seen in severe poisonings. Occasionally cases include a painful urge to urinate and difficulty in breathing. Without administration of atropine, symptoms can persist for many hours depending on the amount consumed.

Amanita muscaria also contains muscimol and ibotenic acid, as does *A. pantherina*, *A. gemmata* and possibly *A. strobiliformis*. Concentrations of toxins are generally higher in *A. pantherina* than in *A. muscaria* and cause more severe cases of poisoning often referred to as Pantherine or Inebriation Syndrome. Symptoms almost always occur between 30 to 120 minutes after ingestion of the fungus, although in unusual cases this can be delayed for up to 6 hours. These include nausea and

vomiting, particularly in children, proceeded by a state of intoxication characterised by incoordination, dizziness, confusion, delirium, and alteration between lethargy, euphoric and manic behaviour. Patients can then fall into a deep 'coma-like' sleep. Hallucinations can occur as well as muscle cramps and spasms and, more rarely, generalised seizures, particularly in younger casualties.

Several species of mushrooms are known to contain hallucinogenic substances, including the *Psilocybe* and *Panaeolus* groups. Some other species of *Conocybe*, *Inocybe* and *Gymnopilus* are also known to contain them. When these species are eaten, psychotropic poisoning is caused by the indole compounds, psilocin and psilocybin that are present in the fruit body. Symptoms are noticeable within 30 minutes after ingestion. These fungi are now considered a Class A drug and it is against the law to be in possession of a fungus containing these substances or to process them in any way. It is not however, an offence to have them growing on your lawn!

Some bracket fungi, such as *Meripilus giganteus* and *Laetiporus sulphureus,* are known to contain unidentified psychotropic alkaloid toxins. Susceptibility to this type of poisoning is extremely variable between individuals. These alkaloids are understood to cause nausea and vomiting in some, but not all, cases. These compounds could be responsible for central nervous system manifestations such as dizziness, and disorientation in others.

Gastrointestinal poisoning can occur from an array of fungi, all of which have some features in common. They provoke symptoms in many, but not all people. They all affect the gastrointestinal tract with various combinations of nausea, vomiting, colicky abdominal pain, and diarrhoea. The toxins are largely unknown. The majority produce symptoms between 15 minutes and 2 hours after ingestion. Two species, *Entoloma sinuatum* and *Paxillus involutus*, have been known to cause fatalities and *Hypholoma fasciculare* has also been known to cause fatal liver damage. *Paxillus involutus* contain antigens which, through cumulative effect by eating more than once, can cause an autoimmune reaction which makes the body attack its own red blood cells. This can lead to fatal kidney and respiratory failure. However most other cases with symptoms lasting 30 minutes to 2 hours require no treatment. Complications can occur in some cases where more than one species is consumed at the same time.

OTHER CAUSES OF POISONINGS

Two other types of fungi poisoning should be mentioned, although occurrences are rare in the UK: *Pleurocybella porrigens*, angel's wings, although previously considered edible, is reported to cause brain injury and fatalities when eaten by people with pre-existing kidney problems. Symptoms appeared 13–18 days after consumption of the mushrooms, which contain a high concentration of unusual amino acids that, due to poor kidney function, cannot be broken down quickly enough when large amounts are consumed. These can reach the brain and cause irreversible damage.

Some species of *Tricholoma*, the knight group, are known, if eaten repeatedly – say three times over two weeks – to cause a delayed onset of rhabdomyolysis, which is a breakdown of skeletal muscle tissue that releases further toxins which can then lead to kidney failure. These species include *Tricholoma equestre,* yellow knight (or knights on horseback, to which it is also sometimes referred) and *Tricholoma terreum,* grey knight. In the tropics, *Russula subnigricans* causes a similar condition but with a more rapid onset of symptoms. *Tricholoma ustale,* burnt knight, has also been implicated in poisoning cases.

Allergic reactions: Toxic symptoms are exhibited in some individuals and not others. There is typically an early onset of symptoms including 'nettle-rash' on skin, headaches and gastroenteritis. Reactions can be quite violent if large quantities are consumed. Cultivated mushrooms and common wild mushrooms such as *Cantharellus cibarius* can cause allergic reactions in the same way that many other foods can. Species to which some people are known to react include *Clitocybe nebularis*, *Lepista nuda* (particularly if not well cooked) and *Chlorophyllum rhacodes*. Fungal spores can also cause allergic reactions as well as being irritants to eyes, and can cause dermatitis.

Contamination: Poisoning can be caused by contamination of mushrooms by herbicides and pesticides, as well as chemicals from contaminated sites such as farmyards and building sites. Road dust and traffic fumes may contain lead and mercury. Fungi readily absorb heavy metals and are susceptible to contamination from radioactive fall-out.

Decomposition: Contamination by microscopic fungi and bacterial infection can occur in decaying mushrooms. This type of food poisoning can be caused by collecting old or partly rotten specimens collecting in plastic bags or closed containers, or through spoilage by incorrect long-term storage. Symptoms are usually gastroenteric and of short duration.

Imaginary poisoning: Fear of fungal poisoning alone can cause some individuals to experience symptoms such as stomachache, nausea and diarrhoea. Panic attacks can induce cold sweats, flushing, dizziness and light-headedness which could be confused with muscarine poisoning, however in this type of case there would be an increase in blood pressure, which is not manifested in the latter syndrome. Panic is not only limited to the potential victim. Parents and others in a position of responsibility, including medical practitioners, can also be susceptible.

FALSE DEATHCAP
Amanita citrina and Amanita citrina var. alba

There are two forms of false deathcap, *Amanita citrina* and *A. citrina* var. *alba* which are now synonymised. Although neither are poisonous, they are reported to have a disagreeable taste and are so easily confused with deathcap (see page 132) that it is best to leave them alone.

IDENTIFICATION
There are two distinct forms of this fungi: one with a pale greenish yellow tinge to the cap (*A. citrina* var. *citrina*) and the other with a pure white cap (*A. citrina* var. *alba*). In both forms the cap is 5–12cm/2–4½in across. It is usually covered with patches of the veil, one of the features that distinguishes it from the deathcap, which rarely has any veil remnants. The stem is 6–11cm/2½–4¼in long and 0.5–1cm/¼–½in wide. It has a large marginate bulb or cup where the remnants of the veil can be seen, and it has a clear ring or skirt around the stem. The gills are free, off-white, darkening with age. The flesh and spore print are white.

Above: False death cap grows in both coniferous and deciduous woodlands. The pure white form is commonly found under beech, but the raw potato-like smell is less pronounced.

Left: In this example, the prominent flat white patches of veil have washed off the cap, leaving it quite smooth.

HABITAT AND SEASON

Amanita citrina typically grows in deciduous or coniferous woods, especially under oak and beech trees. It is more usually found on alkaline or neutral soils, less so on acidic ground. The season is from summer to late autumn. It is unfortunately quite common. Typically this mushroom has a strong smell of raw potatoes, sometimes described as 'earthy radish'. The smell is important because the species it can be confused with, destroying angel and death cap (pale and white form), have a nauseous sweet honey smell which is very indicative.

Right: The cap is typically cream to pale yellow with a patchy surface from the veil remnants.

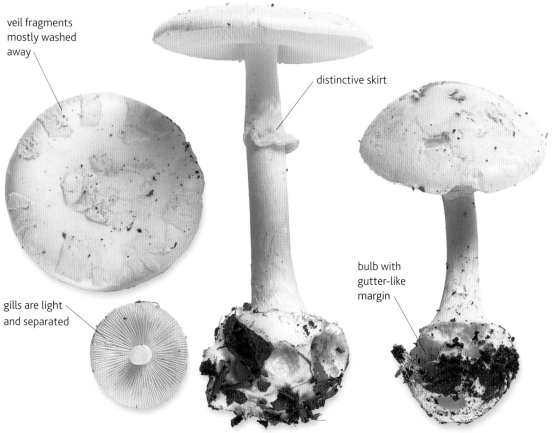

veil fragments mostly washed away

distinctive skirt

gills are light and separated

bulb with gutter-like margin

FLY AGARIC
Amanita muscaria

Without doubt this is everybody's idea of a toadstool or poisonous mushroom. The little flecks on the red cap, which sometimes grows to 20cm/8in across, make it quite distinctive. Many fables of myth and magic are associated with this mushroom. One, which sounds like a myth but is not, is its use by the Sami people of Lapland to round up their reindeer herds. They take advantage of the reindeers' liking for fly agaric and scatter dried ones for the reindeer to eat, which makes them more manageable. The toxins contained in *Amanita muscaria* attack the central nervous system, producing intoxication, hallucination and a euphoria that is similar to drunkenness. The poison stays in the system for several months but the symptoms generally disappear in 12 hours, although it may take several days to fully recover.

Several colour varients of this mushroom have been described, including with yellow tones to the stem and ring.

IDENTIFICATION
These often occur in fairly large groups at all stages of development. The cap of the fly agaric is 6–20cm/2½–8in across, hemispherical at first then convex, before it flattens right out. Although usually bright scarlet and covered with flecks of veil remnant, the colour may fade in wet weather, and a few come up a fairly pale orange. The white stem is 8–25cm/3–10in long and 1–2.5cm/½–1in wide. If you take a specimen right out of the ground you will see the rounded, swollen stem base. The gills are free, and white. The smell is indistinct. The spore print is white.

remains of universal veil

evidence of partial veil, i.e. ring

white gills do not join the spongy stem

Right: After heavy rain, the flecks wash off the cap of the fly agaric and the red colour fades to orange.

HABITAT AND SEASON

Fly agaric is often found with birch trees, although it can occur with a wide range of trees and in many locations, including spruce plantations. The season is late summer to late autumn and it is very common. Peppery bolete parasitises the mycorrhizae of fly agaric, and they are often found fruiting together.

Right: Three stages of growth. The dramatic appearance of this fungi acts as a visual warning, although some more innocuous-looking mushrooms are even deadlier.

CAESAR MUSHROOM

Amanita cesarea

Found in the forests of continental Europe rather than Britain, this edible russet gold and orange mushroom is included as it is a prized picking, occasionally spotted in a market, and is valued for its sweet chestnut-like taste. If you are picking wild, be sure not to confuse it with *Amanita muscaria*. The young egg-shaped mushroom is enveloped by a universal veil, that temporarily covers the mushroom as it grows. It opens up to a full-cap, revealing a ring and bright yellow, deep and thin gills that are attached to the thin film top. The flesh is yellow.

PANTHERCAP
Amanita pantherina

Although less common than fly agaric, panthercap, too, is severely toxic.

IDENTIFICATION
The cap is 4–10cm/1¼–4in across, almost bronze in colour (never pink), and covered with small pure white flecky remnants of veil. The margin also has remnants of the veil. The stem is 6–10cm/2½–4in long and 1–2cm/½–¾in wide, white with a ring. It has a bulbous base and narrow ring, which comes very low down, forming a distinct free rim around the base. There are usually also one or two belted rings immediately above the bulb. The gills are white and quite broad. The spore print is white.

Above: *Amanita pantherina* has a distinctive pure white veil which covers the cap in concentric evenly spaced remnants.

hemispherical when young, the cap opens as the mushroom matures , eventually becoming quite plane when old

the cap margin is incurved for a long time; the gills are free, quite broad and the gill edge can appear quite woolly floccose

there is a distinct narrow hoop-like ring around the middle of the stem, the upper surface of which is smooth, not striate like many other species of Amanita

one or more rings of tissue around bulb-like base

the cylindrical stem ends with a marginate gutter-like bulb at the base

Right: Beech woods on limestone soils are the favourite habitat of panthercap although it will grow under coniferous trees as well.

Below: Panthercap can be confused with grey-spotted amanita, *Amanita excelsa*, which has two recognised variants *A. excelsa* var. *excelsa*, shown below, and *A. excelsa* var. *spissa*.

HABITAT AND SEASON

Panthercaps grow under both coniferous and deciduous trees. Occasionally this mushroom can be found in calcareous grassland which is unusual for a mycorrhizal fungus, however the presence of rockrose, with which it also associates, explains the mystery. It is quite a rare fungus which occurs more often in England than in Scotland.

AMANITA RUBESCENS

The blusher, *Amanita rubescens,* below, has similarities with panthercap (also known as the 'false blusher'), but it is more often confused with the (possibly poisonous) *A. execlsa* (see left). The blusher has similar features although the flesh will pinken when bruised. Many people do eat the blusher, after first (very) carefully cooking it to remove the toxins, however it requires a very expert eye to distinguish between young specimens so it is best to avoid.

DEATHCAP
Amanita phalloides

Each year deathcaps account for most of the fatal poisonings caused by eating mushrooms. They look fairly innocuous, smell a little of sickly-sweet fermented honey, and can be peeled. However, they are deadly. The range of colours can be dramatic, making identification even more difficult. They can vary from a sickly green to dark brown to pale white, so great care must be taken over identification. If you go on a foray, make sure the foray leader finds one to point out to you. If it is dug out of the ground you will clearly see the volval cup at the base. Take a good look and remember what you see, for a large specimen can kill several people.

Below: The volva at the stem base may be completely hidden under the leaf mould, as seen here – beware!

olive cap may sometimes be white or yellowish

white gills are free from the stem

white, cup-like volva surrounds stem base

white ring

Deathcap deserves its name: it is one of the most deadly fungi known to mankind and it is a common cause of death. Prompt treatment at hospital, however, including fluid management, dialysis and other medical treatments can now save lives once the hospital identifies it as *Amanita* poisoning. The symptoms of poisoning take between 8 and 12 hours to become apparent, but during that time the poison has been attacking the liver and the kidneys. The first signs of poisoning are prolonged sickness and diarrhoea with severe abdominal pains; this is often followed by a period of apparent

Above: Always carefully clear away around the stem base to expose the remains of the volva.

Right: The caps often have a slightly radially streaked or fibrous appearance.

recovery when all seems well. However, death from liver and kidney failure will occur within a few days.

IDENTIFICATION
The cap is 6–16cm/2½–6¼in across. It is quite round at first, flattening with age. It has a smooth, almost shiny surface. The colour is often greenish turning to a rather dirty brown, but beware, in wet weather the cap can become quite pale. The stem is 4–15cm/1½–6in long and 1–2cm/½–¾in wide, and white though can have a grey mottling. There is a large ring which is striate on the upper side. The gills are free and quite crowded; white at first, mature specimens may have an almost clay-pink to clay-buff tinge. The flesh is white with a yellow tinge by the cap, and it smells quite sickly-sweet. The volval cup is quite pronounced. The spore print is white.

Be wary of the early stages when it can look similar to a button mushroom. There is also a pale form of *A. phalloides* which is *A. phalloides* var. *alba*. which can be confused with *A. verna* or *A. virosa*. Apart from being pure white, the features are the same and it is just as deadly.

HABITAT AND SEASON
Widespread in mixed deciduous woodland, especially oak and beech. The season is early summer to late autumn.

DESTROYING ANGEL
Amanita virosa

Like many *Amanitas*, destroying angel grows from a volval cup. It is deadly poisonous and well deserves its name, being white and fatal. The symptoms of the poison are the same as for *Amanita phalloides,* affecting the nervous system, liver and kidneys.

slightly pointed cap

pure white

large, white bag-like volva

Above: The cap of this species often has a distinct hump or blunt point at the centre.

IDENTIFICATION
The cap is 3–12cm/1¼–4½in across; bell-shaped at first, it becomes very irregular when open. It is pure white, though the colour may dull with age, and the cap is smooth and sticky. The shaggy-floccose stem is 6–16cm/2½–6¼in long and 0.6–2cm/¼–¾in wide, and grows from a fairly large volval cup that is not regular at the base, but can clearly be seen with the fungus growing from it. The flesh is white with a sickly-sweet, nauseous honey smell. There is a white ring at the top of the stem which is very fragile and often incomplete. The gills are pure white, as is the spore print.

Above: The fungi is concave at first then opens up to a wide, almost flat cap as it matures.

HABITAT AND SEASON

Grows mainly in mixed deciduous woodland, especially with beech and birch, but has also been found with conifers. It is an uncommon mushroom with a more northerly distribution. The season is usually midsummer to autumn. If you are on a foraging expedition, this is another mushroom that you should ask the leader to point out to you if possible, for once seen you will be unlikely to forget it.

Right: The volva at the base of the stem is an important feature to help distinguish destroying angel. A sickly honey smell is very characteristic.

FOOL'S FUNNEL
Clitocybe rivulosa

This is another innocent-looking and yet severely toxic mushroom that can easily be confused with the edible fairy ring champignon, *Marasmius oreades* (see page 58). Both grow in rings, in similar types of location, and appear at much the same time of the year. Indeed, it is not uncommon for rings of each species to grow within a few metres of each other, so take care. The funnel has quite a distinctive shape but it would probably be a good idea to seek out and study live examples of both to be sure of the differences, before you start picking the fairy ring champignon.

HABITAT AND SEASON
In groups or rings in sandy soil amongst grass, beside paths and roads. The season is late summer to late autumn and it is very common.

IDENTIFICATION
The cap is 1–6cm/½–2½in across; buff to greyish-brown with a rather persistent greyish white powdery bloom or frosting, can be patchy. Cup-shaped at first, it soon flattens out with a small depression in the centre. The margin remains slightly rolled. It is grey and concentric rings are visible. The smell is slightly sweetish.

slightly funnel-shaped cap

although the gills are buff, the spores are white.

gills are crowded

gills run down the stem

smooth silky cap, can look frosted

Right: *Clitocybe rivulosa* mushrooms can be dull to silky white. The margin is always somewhat inrolled and even.

Below: This shows the rather frosted appearance of the creamy-white caps and the slightly decurrent gills.

The stem is 1.5–4cm/½–1½in long and 0.3–0.8cm/about ¼in wide, and a similar colour to the cap.

The crowded, grey gills run part-way down the stem. The flesh is dirty white to grey. The closeness of the gills and the colour and shape of the cap are important ways to distinguish this mushroom from the fairy ring champignon. The spore print is white.

OTHER CLITOCYBES

There are a number of dangerous *Clitocybes* that can look similar, with silky, frosted white or cream caps in a more or less funnel shape, and decurrent gills that run down the stem. The *C. dealbata* (once known as the ivory funnel), below, is now considered to be synonymous with *C. rivulosa*. Care must be taken when picking any white-gilled mushroom that it is not a poisonous *Clitocybe*. The miller, *Clitopilus prunulus* (see page 51), is an edible lookalike, thought to be parasitic on the mycorrhiza of *Boletus edulis* and therefore growing in the same habitat. It is usually avoided except by experts due to risk of misidentification.

DAPPERLINGS
Lepiota species

The dapperling group include some of the most deadly mushrooms that one is likely to encounter. Some species contain amatoxins also found in the deathcap and destroying angel.

STINKING DAPPERLING *Lepiota cristata*
Although stinking dapperlings do not contain amatoxins, they are considered suspect, poisonous and should be avoided, not least because they could be confused with their fatally poisonous relatives. They are quite variable in size and appearance, but very common. The caps, 1.5–7.5cm/½–3in, are bell-shaped to plane, with a distinct brown umbo in the centre which soon breaks up into small concentric scales contrasting against a pale background. The silky white stem, 1.5–7cm/½–2¾in long and 0.2–0.8cm/under ½in wide, is cylindrical with a slightly clavate pink-brown base and a membranous but fragile ring which is often torn or attached to the cap margin. The free gills are medium-spaced and white. It has a strong unpleasant gas-like smell which is sometimes likened to pear drops. The flesh is white; the spore print is white. This mushroom is found on rich soil and litter in deciduous woodland, in scrubland, gardens and on waste ground. It is rarely reported with conifers. Its season is from summer to autumn.

FRECKLED DAPPERLING *Echinoderma asperum*
This is one of the larger dapperling species. It has distinctive brown warts that contrast against the white background colour of the cap. This mushroom is sometimes described as edible or edibility unknown, however it is known to cause problems when consumed with alcohol in a similar way to common inkcap. It has been mistaken for *Amanita rubescens*, blusher; *Macrolepiota procera*, parasol; and young *Agaricus augustus*, the prince. Its cap is 6–18cm/2½–7in, initially conical then soon expanding but often retaining a low umbo, orange-brown to brown in the centre, covered with brown warts radiating to fibrous spines at the margin. The stem, 5–12cm/2–4¾in long and 0.8–1.6cm/around ½in wide, is cylindrical, white above the ring and with woolly brown fibres below. The ring is cottony with occasional brown warts to the underside. The free gills are

Below: Stinking dapperling.

Below: Freckled dapperling.

Above: Deadly dapperling.

Above: Chestnut dapperling.

white to cream, often forking and very crowded. The spore colour is cream/white. Its smell is unpleasant, similar to *Lepiota cristata*. It is mostly found on, but not restricted to, rich soils in broadleaved woodland, occasionally in coniferous woodland, on broad diameter deadwood and in gardens. Its season is from summer to autumn.

DEADLY DAPPERLING *Lepiota brunneoincarnata*
Similar in stature but far darker than stinking dapperlings, deadly dapperlings are considerably less common. *Lepota brunneoincarnata* contains the same amatoxins found in deathcap and destroying angel and is just as deadly. The cap is 2.5–6cm/1–2½in, convex to plane, dark red to purple brown, with a faint purple tinge towards the margin, cracking into concentric rings of scales which contrast against the white flesh of the cap. The stem is 2.5–6cm/1–2½in long and 0.5–1cm/under ½in wide, silky whitish pink at the top, with brown scales below the ring zone towards the base. There is a very ephemeral, short-lived ring. The gills are free and rather crowded, cream to white. The spores are cream/white; the smell is fruity. It is often solitary, on disturbed soil, with deciduous trees or conifers, and also amongst grass on dunes. Its season is summer to autumn.

FATAL DAPPERLING *Lepiota subincarnata*
Very similar-looking to deadly dapperling, fatal dapperling is just as poisonous but is generally paler with rose brown tones in the cap. It is becoming more common, particularly in the south of England. Its cap is 1.5–5cm/½–2in, is convex expanding to plane, sometimes with a low umbo, pink to pale brown surface cracking into scales, becoming paler towards the margin. Veil remains can also sometimes be seen at the margin. The stem, 2–5cm/¾–2in long and 0.2–1cm/under ½in wide, is cylindrical but slightly broadening to the base with white pinkish girdles below the ring zone. Gills are free, white/cream and medium-spaced. The spore colour is cream/white. This mushroom smells fruity but with a farinaceous component. It is found in deciduous woodland edges and increasingly in gardens on lawns and beds. Its season is autumn.

CHESTNUT DAPPERLING *Lepiota castanea*
More richly coloured, this is another autumn member of the very poisonous dapperling group, with gills that bruise orange. It has a richer fruity, cedar-like smell. This is one of the less common dapperlings, known mostly from chalky soils in southern England. There are only two records of it from Scotland.

BEARDED MILKCAP
Lactarius pubescens

A member of the large milkcap family, it is important to be able to identify this mushroom for not only is it a strong emetic but it can be confused with the edible saffron milkcap, *Lactarius deliciosus* (see page 62). The woolly edges of *L. pubescens* are an important distinguishing feature. Equally common and shaggy is *L. torminosus*, a brighter pink and just as upsetting if eaten.

IDENTIFICATION
The cap is 4–10cm/1½–4in across, convex and slightly depressed, with the margin markedly inrolled and woolly at the edge although it can become smooth with age. It is pale cream to flesh-pink, but this tends to fade in direct sunlight. The stem is 4–7cm/1½–2¾in long and 1–2cm/½–¾in wide, and cream to palish pink. The gills are adnate to decurrent, crowded, and cream darkening with age. The gills can run down the stem and produce an abundant white acrid latexy milk. The flesh is quite thick and whitish, but can have a pinkish tinge. There is no fruity smell. The spore print is creamy white.

HABITAT AND SEASON
This mushroom tends to grow fairly widely, always near birch trees on fairly poor or sandy soil. The season is late summer to late autumn.

inrolled cap margin

gills bleed white milk when cut

funnel-shaped cap

LACTARIUS TORMINOSUS
The cap of *Lactarius pubescens* is a pale pinkish white; if the cap is deep pink you may have *L. torminosus*, woolly milkcap, below.

SICKENER
Russula emetica

There are hundreds of different species of *Russula*, making it a large group of fungi which can be hard to identify. Some, such as charcoal burner, are edible, but some are very hot to taste and can cause stomach upsets. Sickener and the very similar-looking beechwood sickener, *R. nobilis*, did not get their names without good reason. It is best to avoid these bright red, very acrid-tasting brittlegills.

IDENTIFICATION
The cap is 3–10cm/1¼–4in across and is cup-shaped, later flattening with a shallow central depression. The cap is a brightish red, but often has faded white areas. When peeled, it shows red-coloured flesh underneath. The white stem is 5–8cm/2–3in long and 1–2cm/½–¾in wide. The gills are whitish, darkening slightly with age. The flesh is fragile and can be quite sticky. It is white except under the cap. The spore print is white.

Above: Sickener is typically found under pines, especially in wet areas.

HABITAT AND SEASON
Grows under pines and broadleaf trees. The season is summer to late autumn and it is very common. As its name suggests, beechwood sickener, which has a similar season, grows exclusively under beech trees.

pure white stem and gills

flesh is brittle and crumbly

widely spaced gills

red cap skin peels off very easily

POISONPIE
Hebeloma crustulineforme

Originally thought to be one of the most common of the *Hebeloma* genus, it turns out that *Hebeloma crustuliniforme* is in fact quite rare in Britain. However, there are so many species in the group that look similar in the field, that only microscopic characters can separate them. Species within the group often have a radish-like or sweetish smell and some species exude water droplets on the gills upon which spores coalesce to make them look as though they have brown spots. This mushroom causes severe gastroenteritis.

Poisonpie could be confused with St George's mushrooms or species in the *Agaricus* group, however St George's are late spring mushrooms with white spores and the Agaricus group has dark chocolate-brown spores, so the milky coffee-coloured spores, radish smell and pale gills should easily separate these species. Some people refer to it by another common name, fairy cakes, which is misleading.

IDENTIFICATION
The cap is 2–10cm/¾–4in across, convex, a whitish beige-pink, viscid when wet, and often with a slight wavy crenulated margin, not hygrophanous. The white stem is 2.7–7cm/1–2¾in long and 0.5–1.5cm/¼–½in wide, cylindrical, sometimes broader at the base. Covered by transverse woolly tufts, particularly at the apex becoming hollow with age. Cortina is evident when young. Gills are emarginate, crowded with conspicuous droplets, cream-pink when young, later pink-brown, with a woolly white edge. The flesh colour is white to cream, and it smells strongly of radish. The spore print is a milky coffee-brown.

HABITAT AND SEASON
Common and widespread in broadleaved woodland particularly with birch, and occasionally in coniferous woodland. Its season is summer to autumn.

Left: Look out for brown spots on the gills, which indicate the spore colour and are characteristic of this group..

DEADLY FIBRECAP
Inosperma erubescens

Previously known as *Inocybe erubescens/ patouillardii* (red-staining inocybe). Deadly fibrecap is rare but severely toxic and must not be eaten. There is a danger that it can appear superficially similar to edible *Agaricus* in its first stages. There are 15 species of fibrecap in Britain which show reddening in various parts of the fruitbody in some way. *Inosperma erubescens* is one of the larger, more robust species.

IDENTIFICATION
The cap is 4–10cm/1½–4in across, slightly conical and uneven. The margins are often cracked. Cream-coloured, the cap has red-staining radial fibres. The stem is 4–7cm/1½–2¾in long and 0.8–1.5cm/¼–½in wide, fairly thick and slightly bulbous at the base. The gills are pale buff at first, like those of field mushrooms, then darken to a light brown colour, often with reddish spots. The flesh is white and has a disagreeable smell, reminiscent of

OTHER FIBRECAPS
All of the fibrecap group are poisonous, if not as deadly as this one, and it is best to avoid all the *Inocybes*. Common specimens you might encounter include the white fibrecap (*I. geophylla*) and the lilac fibrecap (*I. geophylla* var. *lilacina*), shown below. They share characteristically radially fibrous caps, often but not always cracked, and a dull brown spore print.

perfumed soap. The spore print is dull brown.

HABITAT AND SEASON
Grows in open woodland on alkaline chalky soils, especially under beech, hazel, oak, birch and lime. A summer species, appearing as early as June but rarely lasting into autumn. This mushroom mainly grows in the south of England.

Left: The white fibrous cap and stem have blood-red stains when bruised. The edges often split with age.

DEADLY WEBCAP
Cortinarius rubellus

Deadly poisonous, this mushroom has been confused both with chanterelle which has wrinkles or folds and not gills, and cep, which has pores on the underside. A reasonable level of scrutiny however should clearly separate these species.

Deadly webcaps are found in coniferous woodlands, mostly with pine, in Scotland and occasionally elsewhere although are thought to be widespread. The very similar fool's webcap, *Cortinarius orellanus,* is found in broadleaved woodland, mainly under oak, and is a rare species (listed as vulnerable). Both are extremely toxic mushrooms which cause kidney failure after a delayed onset of initial symptoms which usually appear between 12 and 48 hours after consumption. In some years, the fruiting of this mushroom can be quite prolific, particularly in plantation woodland.

IDENTIFICATION
The cap is 3–8cm/1¼–3in across, conical then later convex, acutely umbonate, a foxy red-brown to orange-brown in colour, minutely hairy to finely scaly but not hygrophanous. The stem is 5–13cm/2–5¼in long and 07–1.5cm/¼–½in wide, sometimes cylindrical, sometimes tapering to a pointed base; in colour ochraceous-yellow then red-brown. Cortina and universal veil are yellow, distinct against the darker stem.

The gills are adnate, distant and broad, red-brown in colour. The flesh is red-brown and smells faintly of radish. The spore print is a rusty brown.

HABITAT AND SEASON
Found in northern pinewoods, particularly Caledonian pine forest, but also known from sitka spruce plantations.

Left: The matt silky brown cap and stem with fox/rust belts of veil are distinctive of this mushroom. Younger specimens will have the web-like veil intact between the edge of the cap and the stem.

FUNERAL BELL
Galerina marginata

Funeral bell (also called deadly galerina or autumn skullcap, and known as *Galerina autumnalis* in North America) is highly poisonous and to be avoided at all costs.

Above: The brownish-yellow gills distinguish the funeral bell from species such as honey fungus; though the gills of honey fungus often darken in age, they will have white spores.

IDENTIFICATION
The cap is 0.5–3cm/¼–1¼in across though can be larger, up to 7cm/2¾in. It is convex at first, becoming flatter to slightly depressed, rarely with a slight dome at the centre. It is hygrophanous, yellow-brown to red-brown drying paler, and when moist is quite sticky and shiny. The stem is 2–7cm/¾–2¾in long and 0.2–0.5cm/under ¼in wide, cylindrical to slightly thicker at the base, and silky white below the ring zone. There are slight brownish to blackish markings at the base of the stem, and the mycelial threads are clearly visible at the bottom. There is a ring that breaks fairly easily and is quite small. The gills are adnate or with a small decurrent tooth, yellowish becoming redder with age. The flesh is off-white and smells slightly mealy. The spore print is ochre to rusty brown.

HABITAT AND SEASON
A common mushroom that tends to live on well-decayed coniferous wood but also appears on larger trunks of deciduous wood, as well as in grassland and heaths occasionally. These mushrooms contain amatoxins.

BROWN ROLLRIM
Paxillus involutus

Brown rollrim (also once known as poison paxillus) is a very common mushroom. It is also severely toxic. It can have a boletus-like shape, which makes matters worse, as some boletus species, of course, are considered edible. Toxins cause the body to attack its own red blood cells, leading to fatal kidney and respiratory failure.

Above: A central dip, rolled grooved margin and decurrent gills are distinctive features.

Below: Immature cap with tightly rolled cap margin.

IDENTIFICATION
The cap size is 4–15cm/1½–6in across. It is quite flat when young, becoming convex and somewhat funnel-shaped with age. It gets its name from its clearly inrolled rim, and ochre to yellow/rust brown colour. The cap is slippery when moist, shiny when dry. The stem is up to 4–10cm/1½–4in long and 1–2.5cm/½–1in wide, and similar in colour to the cap. The

crowded gills
run down
the stem

inrolled margin

narrow decurrent gills are yellow, turning brown to red-brown when bruised. The spore print is olive-brown.

HABITAT AND SEASON
The brown rollrim grows beside paths in broad-leaved woodland, especially with birch, and on quite acid scrubland. It has a long growing season from summer to late autumn.

Above right: The cap margin remains inrolled, even when mature.

Right: The gills stain a characteristic brown when bruised, and are easily separated from the flesh of the cap with either a scrape of a knife or fingernail.

YELLOW STAINER
Agaricus xanthodermus

Yellow stainers account for a large proportion of the cases of mushroom poisoning among those who pick either field or horse mushrooms. They have an unpleasant smell and taste, and must be avoided at all costs. The symptoms of poisoning are sweating and flushing with unpleasant stomach cramps. Not everyone is affected by yellow stainer, but it is not worth taking any risks – leave it well alone. Unfortunately identification of this mushroom can be difficult as it can be quite varied in its size and colour, and the cap can range from smooth to scaly, so it is important to take careful note of its key distinguishing features.

IDENTIFICATION
The cap is 6–15cm/2½–6in across. Convex and angular at first, it flattens out later with a dip in the centre. Very white when young, it darkens with age as it expands to a fairly large cap with greyish brown scales. It bruises a very bright yellow as soon as it is touched, scratched or cut, making this a valuable identification feature. Although this mushroom has many similarities with other members of the Agaric family, the bright yellow staining is the giveaway, especially at the base of the stem, which does not occur with the horse and macro mushrooms. The stem is 6–12.5cm/2½–5in long and 1–2cm/½–¾in

intense yellow stains when scratched, fading to brown

expands to a large cap which sometimes has dark scales

thick ring joins cap to stem

white at first, mature gills turn pink then brown

stem will bruise yellow when cut

cap can become greyish and slightly scaly with age

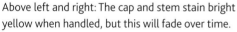
Above left and right: The cap and stem stain bright yellow when handled, but this will fade over time.

wide, often slightly bulbous at the base, and white, staining bright yellow at the base. The gills are crowded, free and remote from the stem, pink at first then grey and finally dark brown with age. The flesh is white. Smell is an important means of identifying this mushroom as it smells something like carbolic. The spore print is dark chocolate-brown. Should you have picked a yellow stainer by mistake and put it in your pan it will quite often turn the rest of the contents a slimy sickly yellow. It will also give off a very unpleasant acrid smell in the kitchen.

HABITAT AND SEASON
Yellow stainer grows in woods, pastures and gardens. It has a long growing season, summer to late autumn. It is common in certain areas.

LOOKALIKE
Related to yellow stainer, *Agaricus moelleri* or inky mushroom is another potential lookalike for edible mushrooms such as the prince, blushing wood mushroom or wood mushroom, and similar to other *Agaricus* at different stages of growth.

COMMON INKCAP
Coprinopsis atramentaria

Although common inkcap is not poisonous in itself, if eaten in conjunction with alcohol, it can cause alarming symptoms, such as nausea, palpitations and stomach cramps. For this reason it has been used over the years in the past to cure alcoholics. Inkcap gets its name from the fact that it was used many years ago by monks to produce an exceptionally fine drawing ink, made by boiling the collapsed inky caps with a little water and a hint of cloves. The difference between common inkcap and edible shaggy inkcap (see page 80) is quite marked, but it is important that you recognise this one for it would be a catastrophe to make a mistake at a dinner party at which you were serving alcohol. Young specimens of magpie inkcap, *Coprinopsis picacea*, could also be confused with common inkcap. While not as common as this, it grows in fairly large quantities in the late summer to autumn. It is best avoided because, although not poisonous, it can cause nausea and vomiting in some people.

gills blacken and liquefy when mature from the edge inwards

fine ring zone in the lower part of the stem

brown scaly base to stem

Below: The inkcap is frequently seen in town parks, gardens and woodlands. Specimens can grow quite close together, often in large groups.

IDENTIFICATION
The cap is 3–6cm/1¼–2½in across, white, conical and later bell-shaped. Light grey to greyish-brown in colour, with veil remnants often attached to the cap. The stem is 5–17cm/2–6½in long and 1–1.5cm/about ½in wide, smooth and white, with a ring zone towards the base. The gills are crowded, white at first, changing from brown to a dark inky mass. The smell is not distinctive. The spore print is dark brown to black.

HABITAT AND SEASON
Grows in tufts, often in association with dead or buried wood. The season is from spring to late autumn and they are very common.

SULPHUR TUFT
Hypholoma fasciculare

This common mushroom grows all the year round. It can be deadly poisonous and definitely should be avoided. It could be confused with other poisonous fungi, such as funeral bell (page 145), but also edible mushrooms such as velvet shank (page 52) and honey fungus (pages 42–43). Another edible, *Hypholoma lateritium* or brick tuft, is also avoided due to its similarity.

black spores can be observed at the ring zone at the top of the stem or on the surface of other caps below

IDENTIFICATION

The cap is 1–6cm/½–2½in across and is convex. Remains of the veil often adhere to the margin. The cap is orange when young, later sulphur yellow with a dark orange centre, and is not hygrophanous. The stem is 3–8cm/1¼–3¼in long and 0.2–0.8cm/under ¼in wide, curved and a similar colour to the cap. The stems are joined at the base. The gills are crowded, a bright yellow, tinged greenish-yellow, finally turning purplish-brown to black. The flesh is yellow, becoming browner near the base of the stem. It has a quinine smell and is very bitter. The spore print is purple-black.

HABITAT AND SEASON

This mushroom occurs in dense clusters on the rotting timber and stumps of deciduous and occasionally coniferous trees. It grows throughout the year, even in the winter. It is very common, and easily identified by its grey-green gills and sulphur cap.

Right: Found on dead or dying wood, sulphur tuft grows in large clumps, growing in bundles or 'fascicules'.

FURTHER READING

It is a good idea to have a broad reference library to refer to. This list includes some old classics as well as more recent guides. Note that older editions may have earlier taxonomy, as classification does change over time, and as new research is shared.

No general book can be a detailed guide to all the fungi to be found in your locality. Try to hunt out relevant regional mushroom field guides as very useful additions to your library.

There are also websites of course, some more reputable than others. As with books, do not rely on visual recognition as a sole means of identification; even if the image is correctly labelled (which it might not be), mushrooms can look markedly different depending on age, season, location, sub-species and many other factors.

Do look out for local foraging expeditions as the guidance from an expert is invaluable experience.

Benjamin, D., *Mushrooms: poisons and panaceas,* W. H. Freeman and Company 1995

Boertmann, D., *The Genus Hygrocybe*, 2nd revised edition, Jens H. Petersen/Low Budget Publishing 2010

Carluccio, A., *A Passion for Mushrooms*, Pavilion Books 1990

Clowez, P. & Moreau, P., *Morels of Europe*, Cap Régions Éditions 2021

Dann, G., *Edible Mushrooms*, Green Books (UIT Cambridge Ltd) 2017

Dickenson, Colin and Lucas, John, ed., *The Encyclopedia of Mushrooms*, Putnam 1979

Findlay, W. P. K., *Wayside and Woodland Fungi*, Frederick Warne 1967

Garnweidner, E., *Mushrooms and Toadstools of Britain and Europe*, Collins 1981

Hurst, J. and Rutherford, L., *A Gourmet's Guide to Mushrooms and Truffles*, HP Books 1991

Hyams, M., and O'Keefe, L., *The Mushroom Cookbook*, Lorenz Books 2017

Lincoff, G. H. and Parioni, G. (ed.), *Simon and Schuster's Guide to Mushrooms*, Simon and Schuster 1981

Kibby, G., *An Illustrated Guide to Mushrooms and Other Fungi of Britain and Northern Europe*, Parkgate Books 1997

Kibby, G., *The Genus Agaricus in Britain*, 2011

Kibby, G., *The Genus Amanita in Britain*, 2012

Knudsen, H. & Vesterholt, J. (eds), *Funga Nordica*, Nordsvamp, Copenhagen 2008

Legon & Henrici, *Checklist of the British & Irish Basidiomycota*, RBG Kew, Richmond 2005

Læssøe, T. & Petersen, J. *Fungi of Temperate Europe,* Princeton University Press 2019

Oldridge, S. G., Pegler, D. N. & Spooner, B. M., *Wild Mushroom and Toadstool Poisoning*, RBGK 1989

Pegler, D. N. & Watling, R., *British Toxic Fungi*, Bull. Br. Mycol. Soc. Vol 16 (1): 66-75, 1982

Phillips, R., *Mushrooms,* Macmillan 2006

Phillips, R., *Mushrooms and Other Fungi of Great Britain and Europe*, Pan Books 1981

Stevenson, G., *Field Guide to Fungi*, University of Canterbury Publication No. 30, 1982

Watling, R, *Children and Toxic Fungi*, RBGE, 1995

Wright, John, *River Cottage Handbook Mushrooms*, Bloomsbury, 2007

www.basidiochecklist.info/Names.asp
www.buckandbirch.com
www.gallowaywildfoods.com
www.indexfungorum.org/Names/Names.asp
www.mycokey.com/
www.mycobank.org
www.nhbs.com/1/series/british-fungus-flora-agarics-and-boleti
sites.google.com/site/scottishfungi/

INDEX

Page numbers in **bold** denote the featured mushrooms, including photographs. Other photographs are shown in *italic*.

ACKNOWLEDGEMENTS

Published by Lorenz Books
an imprint of Anness Publishing Ltd
www.lorenzbooks.com; info@anness.com

© Anness Publishing Ltd 2024

Publisher: Joanna Lorenz
Contributing author and editor: Neville Kilkenny
Original author: Peter Jordan
Design: Nigel Partridge
Illustrations: Penny Brown
Index: Elizabeth Wise
Production: Ben Worley

IMAGES: With thanks to Alamy: 57bl, 60bl, 75, 101tl; Dreamstime: 139r; Shutterstock: 12bl, 12br, 13tc, 14tr, 14br, 15bl, 15br, 28bl, 29bl, 38, 43tr, 47t, 48, 51b, 54bl, 54br, 55tl, 55tr, 56tr, 57tr, 57br, 62b, 63t, 63b, 64t, 67b, 71tl, 71tr, 71br, 76t, 77l, 81b, 84t, 88t, 89b, 92b, 93b, 95bl, 101tr, 104b, 105b, 106tl, 107t, 107b, 108b, 111bl, 113tr, 113bl, 115t, 115br, 117t, 118, 120, 123tl, 123tc, 123bc, 123bl, 123br, 127t, 129b, 130tr, 130bl, 131t, 131bl, 131br, 134l, 135t, 135b, 138l, 139r, 140br, 142, 143tr, 145, 146t, 147b, 149tl, 149tr; Wiki: 13br (Kineticcrusher), 129t (Onderwijsgek), 137t (Andreas Kunze), 137c (Strobilomyces), 138r, 143bl (both Andreas Kunze); Neville Kilkenny: 2, 4tl, 4br, 5, 6, 14bl, 15tr, 28br, 29br, 30l, 40, 42, 45, 46bl, 49t, 52t, 53, 58, 61t, 69bl, 69br, 72t, 77r, 78t, 79, 82bl, 86bl, 87br, 88b, 91b, 92t, 93t, 96bl, 96tr, 99br, 102, 103b, 104t, 106br, 109tr, 109bl, 109br, 111tl, 111tr, 116l, 123tr, 126r, 132bl, 134r, 137b, 139l, 144, 149br, 150bl, 151b, 160; Jon Ashford for Anness Publishing Ltd: 10tr, 26, 32–34; all other images: Peter Henley for Anness Publishing Ltd.

ABOUT THE AUTHORS

Peter Jordan spent many years running a world-renowned pub in rural Norfolk, England, where he devoted his time to collecting mushrooms and foraging workshops.

Neville Kilkenny is a consultant mycologist, running many foraging expeditions and workshops. Based in Scotland, he is also a professional carpenter and experienced in bushcraft skills.

FUNGI FORAYING

One of the best ways to learn about mushrooms is to go on a foray led by an expert. You should aim to learn one or two species at a time and gain confidence with them before moving on. Next time you join a led foray, you can get to know two more and so over a relatively short period of time you can develop a broad repertoire of species with which you are familiar. Not only will you have the chance to question the expert about the habitat preferences, time of year and lookalikes for each species you find, but at the end of the foray you will get the chance to examine what everyone else has found and discover their identity too. In this way you will have an opportunity to learn about far more species than you would have if you had just gone out collecting on your own. Forays are run by many organisations, including mycological societies, fungus recording groups, local nature trusts and local experts with events running throughout the year.

NOTE: The advice and information in this book are believed to be accurate and true at the time of going to press, but neither the author nor the publisher can accept legal responsibility or liability for any errors or omissions nor for any loss, harm or injury that may occur.